CHILDREN CROSSING BORDERS

CHILDREN CROSSING BORDERS

Immigrant Parent and Teacher Perspectives on Preschool

Joseph Tobin,
Angela E. Arzubiaga,
and Jennifer Keys Adair

Russell Sage Foundation
New York

The Russell Sage Foundation

The Russell Sage Foundation, one of the oldest of America's general purpose foundations, was established in 1907 by Mrs. Margaret Olivia Sage for "the improvement of social and living conditions in the United States." The Foundation seeks to fulfill this mandate by fostering the development and dissemination of knowledge about the country's political, social, and economic problems. While the Foundation endeavors to assure the accuracy and objectivity of each book it publishes, the conclusions and interpretations in Russell Sage Foundation publications are those of the authors and not of the Foundation, its Trustees, or its staff. Publication by Russell Sage, therefore, does not imply Foundation endorsement.

Library of Congress Cataloging-in-Publication Data

Tobin, Joseph Jay.
  Children crossing borders : immigrant parent and teacher perspectives on preschool / Joseph Tobin, Jennifer Keys Adair, and Angela Arzubiaga.
    pages cm
  Includes bibliographical references and index.
  ISBN 978-0-87154-799-6 (pbk. : alk. paper)—ISBN 978-1-61044-807-9 (ebook) 1. Children of immigrants—Education (Early childhood)—United States. 2. Immigrants—Education—United States. I. Title.
  LC3746.T63 2013
  371.826'9120973—dc23   2013018572

RUSSELL SAGE FOUNDATION
112 East 64th Street, New York, New York 10065
10 9 8 7 6 5 4 3 2 1

Contents

Tables   vii

About the Authors   ix

Preface and Acknowledgments   xi

Chapter 1   Introduction   1

Chapter 2   Community Contexts and Research Methods   20

Chapter 3   Curriculum   35

Chapter 4   Language   59

Chapter 5   Identity   79

Chapter 6   Facilitating Dialogue   117

References   129

Index   141

Tables

Table 2.1   Focus Group Interviews with Staff: School/
             Participant Characteristics   29

Table 2.2   Focus Group Interviews with Parents: School/
             Participant Characteristics   31

About the Authors |

JOSEPH TOBIN is the Elizabeth Garrard Hall Professor of Early Childhood Education at the University of Georgia.

ANGELA E. ARZUBIAGA is associate professor in the School of Social Transformation at Arizona State University.

JENNIFER KEYS ADAIR is assistant professor of curriculum and instruction at the University of Texas at Austin.

Preface and Acknowledgments |

"CHILDREN CROSSING BORDERS" began as an idea for a collaborative international research project in 2002 when my French colleagues, Gilles Brougère and Sylvia Rayna, and I decided to do a comparative international study of approaches to early childhood and care among countries in Europe. Gilles, Sylvie, and I invited Chris Pascal and Tony Bertram to join us as the England research team leaders. When Chris and Tony suggested that the study focus on how early childhood education programs in each country are dealing with migration, we enthusiastically agreed. With this in mind, we decided to add Germany, a country whose approach to immigration, we felt, would provide a useful contrast to both France's republicanism (Brougère, Guénif-Souilamas, and Rayna 2008) and England's version of multiculturalism; Christa Preissing came on board as leader of the Berlin-based German team. We then decided to add Italy as a fourth country, both because of the excellent reputation of Italy's preschools and because we felt that Italy, as a country relatively new to receiving immigrants, would provide a useful counterpoint; Susanna Mantovani joined the project as the Italian team leader.

The last country we added to the study was the United States, the self-proclaimed land of immigrants. I invited my colleague at Arizona State University, Angela Arzubiaga, to be my co-principal investigator on the U.S. research and my then-doctoral student, Jennifer Adair, to be the U.S. research coordinator. Angela eventually became the PI for the U.S. research as I put more of my energy into running the larger international project. Jennifer became increasingly responsible for the management and analysis of the data.

Angela, Jennifer, and I gradually came to the realization that the data from the United States were sufficiently rich and complicated to warrant their own book. Although this book is only about the United States, our research questions, methods, conceptual framework, and organization of findings reflect the fruits of our close collaboration with our European colleagues. The Children Crossing Borders research team met frequently from 2004 to 2009, in both the United States and Europe. These meetings, our email correspondence in between them, and our collaborative conference presentations and authorship of papers were invaluable to the development of the ideas in this book.

We want to acknowledge the contributions of each member of the research team: Fikriye Kurban worked closely with me coordinating the international project and collaborating with the country teams on shooting and editing the videos. Tamara Fuster, a graduate assistant on the U.S. team, played a major role in the intervention stage of the project, described in chapter 6, and she helped draft an earlier version of that chapter. Ana Morales Santiago and Lirio Patton were interviewers on the U.S. team. During a sabbatical year he spent with us in Arizona, Gilles Brougère helped to facilitate focus groups in Nuevo Campo, Iowa, and Nashville, Tennessee, and conducted a focus group in French in New York City with West African immigrants.

Dalvir Gill joined Tony Bertram and Chris Pascal on the English team. Christa Preissing's German research team included Petra Wagner, Annika Sulzer, and Anja Jungen. Nacira Guénif-Souilamas joined Gilles Brougère and Sylvie Rayna as leaders of the French team, and Nathalie Thomauske came on as a research assistant for both the French and German teams. Chiara Bove joined Susanna Mantovani as co-PI of the Italian team, which also included the graduate research assistants Giulia Pastori and Francesca Zaninelli.

At the inception of the project, our Belgian friend Michel Vandenbroeck introduced us to Henriette Heimgaertener, who at the time was a program officer at the Bernard van Leer Foundation. With Henriette's encouragement, we developed a proposal to BvLF, which funded the international organization of the project. Our English colleagues secured funding from the Esmée Fairburn Foundation for the U.K. portion of the research. The Spencer Foundation awarded us a major grant for the U.S. research, and I was invited by the Russell Sage Foundation to spend a year in New York as a visiting scholar to work on this book. We are grateful to all three of these funders for investing in this research.

In addition to acting as matchmaker between our team and the Bernard van Leer Foundation, Michel Vandenbroeck gave us valuable advice at various junctures, and in this book we draw heavily on his trenchant analyses of the complexities of the interactions between immigrant parents and their children's teachers. An early version of our findings was published in a book edited by Celia Genishi, who gave us valuable feedback and introduced us to possible research sites. During my year in New York

City, I was able to participate in a study group at New York University organized by Fabienne Doucet, whose own scholarship on immigrant parents and preschools has had a significant impact on our understandings. I benefited from a year of intellectual engagement with the other visiting scholars at RSF during my tenure there in 2007. Back in Arizona, Norma Gonzalez gave us support and encouragement, and we have drawn heavily on her work with Luis Moll and Kathy Amanti on "Funds of Knowledge." Bruce Fuller gave us useful feedback as a discussant on a panel where we presented our earlier findings. Gail Boldt helped us set up the Iowa research sites and even pitched in as a focus group facilitator, with her doctoral student Karen Wohlwend, on an evening when we were shorthanded.

Angela Arzubiaga, Jennifer Adair, and I worked very closely together on all phases of the U.S. research, from writing the Spencer grant proposal to traveling around the country conducting focus group interviews, to analyzing the resulting transcripts, to collaboratively writing this book. We dedicate this book to our children, each one of whom had the experience of being a border crosser when young: Sam and Isaac Tobin; Berkeley, Atticus, and Gideon Adair; and Antonella Artiles Arzubiaga.

Joseph Tobin
University of Georgia

Chapter 1 | Introduction

AT THE CONCLUSION OF A DISCUSSION we ran with a group of nine Mexican mothers at a Head Start program on New York's Upper West Side, we asked if there was anything they wanted us to communicate to their children's teachers. One mother replied: "Ask them, 'Would it kill you to teach my child to write her name before she enters kindergarten?'" Later that day we interviewed the program's African American director:

TOBIN: In the focus groups here, many of the immigrant parents told us that they want more direct instruction and academic emphasis. Are you aware of this?

DIRECTOR: Yes, of course. We hear this all the time.

TOBIN: What would you say to the idea that you should change your approach to be closer to what the parents want?

DIRECTOR: "We shall not be moved."

This is a particularly stark and eloquent example of a pattern we found in the research we conducted in preschools in sites across the United States: immigrant parents and early childhood educators often have differing notions of what should happen in preschool.

For most young children of parents who have come to the United States from another country, preschool is the first and most profound context in which they come face to face with differences between the culture of home and the public culture of their new country. For parents who have recently immigrated to a new country, enrolling their child in a preschool program is the paradigmatic moment when the cultural values of their home and their adopted culture come into contact and, sometimes, conflict. And for the United States and other countries with high rates of immigration, preschools are key sites for the creation of new citizens.

One in four children under age six in the United States has at least one immigrant parent and speaks a language other than English at home (Capps et al. 2005). In many school districts, a majority of students enrolled in public preschool programs are children of recent immigrants. And yet most preschool directors and teachers are given little guidance on how best to serve the immigrant children and families who come through their doors. In the absence of effective programs for bridging the worlds of home and school, new immigrant parents struggle to figure out what is expected of them, what role they can play in their child's preschool, if any, and how they might voice their wishes and concerns. And three- and four-year-old children are left with the task of being border crossers—moving back and forth each day between the often discordant cultural worlds of home and school.

With these issues in mind, we joined colleagues from England, France, Germany, and Italy to initiate the "Children Crossing Borders" research project. This research focused on the contrasting views of recent immigrants and the teachers who educate and care for their children on the means and ends of early childhood education. This book is a report on the U.S. portion of the larger study.

Our chosen method for this study was video-cued multi-sited ethnography (Tobin, Wu, and Davidson 1989). We made a videotape of a typical day in a preschool classroom that served four-year-old immigrant children and then used this video as a cue for focus group interviews with parents and teachers across varied settings—from small towns to large cities, and from communities with a long history of being immigrant gateways to communities in which immigration was a recent phenomenon. This study is the first to systematically compare the beliefs and perspectives of immigrant parents and the preschool practitioners who teach their children. It is also the first to employ a multi-sited ethnographic design to compare how parent and teacher perspectives on immigration play out in a variety of community contexts around the country: urban, suburban, and rural neighborhoods in and around Phoenix, Arizona; Nuevo Campo (the pseudonym we have given to a small town on the border of Arizona and Sonora, Mexico); an Iowa farming community we call "Riverdale"; urban and semi-urban neighborhoods in Nashville; and two neighborhoods in New York, one on the Upper West Side at a Head Start center, where most of the children come from Spanish-speaking homes, and the other in Harlem, where a church-based Head Start preschool serves a mixture of low-income African Americans and new immigrants from West

Africa and the West Indies. In chapter 2, we describe each of the research settings and explain how we carried out the research and the logic that informs our method.

THE INTERSECTION OF IMMIGRATION AND EARLY CHILDHOOD EDUCATION

Debates about strategies for incorporating new immigrants into the fabric of American society and the role of preschools in this process have been going on for more than a century. Indeed, the origins of American early childhood education and care programs can be traced back in part to the urban settlement house preschools opened at the turn of the twentieth century to serve the children of recent immigrants from Europe. From its beginnings, early childhood education in the United States has been focused on providing children of recent immigrants with the kind of education and socialization that they need to become productive American citizens (Lissak 1983, 1989). Working from a deficit model, a central assumption of many of the first early childhood education programs in New York, Chicago, and other gateway cities was that recent immigrants are ill prepared to raise American children (Beatty 1997; Berg 2010; Fass 2006).

Rivka Lissak (1989) suggests that in that period there were two opposing paradigms for the early education of immigrants. Jane Addams espoused a respect for the cultural heritages of the families served in the Hull House nursery and sympathy with the immigrants' plight. In contrast, Robert A. Woods, the founder of the South End House in Boston, championed an approach that "considered 'new immigrants' a menace to the homogeneity, national solidarity, and inherent nature of the Anglo-American civilization," and therefore he advocated aggressively assimilationist strategies (Lissak 1989, 4–5). Lissak suggests that even in Addams's progressive, pro-immigrant approach there was a tension between respectfully supporting the maintenance of the values and practices of children's home cultures and creating a "cross-fertilization" (8) that would lead to a desirable withering of patterns of ethnic-cultural uniqueness and to a "harmonized-holist society" (13).

We cite this early twentieth-century history of immigration and early childhood education in the United States to emphasize that policy divides about how best to educate and socialize young immigrant children reflect deep, long-standing, unresolved tensions in American society. In the contemporary period, the goal of Americanization in early childhood education programs continues to coexist, in uneasy tension, with the goals of maintaining cultural heritages and celebrating diversity (Arzubiaga, Noguerón, and Sullivan 2009; Lightfoot 2004; Souto-Manning 2007).

THE BATTLEGROUND ISSUES

Language

One of the most heated debates about immigration and early education concerns language policy. After decades of calls to develop bilingual education programs to help young children learn English while maintaining their heritage language and connection to their heritage culture, the pendulum has swung in the other direction, toward English-language immersion programs and an emphasis on preschools as sites to get children of recent immigrants and other young children defined as "at risk" off to a good start academically. The English-language-only policies passed first in California and then in Arizona and other states apply mostly to K-12 classrooms, but their impact on preschool programs has been felt in the greater pressure put on staff and parents to have children fluent in English before they enter kindergarten (Arzubiaga and Adair 2009). One result has been a decline in bilingual programs (Dyson 2003; Evans and Hornberger 2005; Fillmore 1991; Genishi and Goodwin 2008). In chapter 4, we explore immigrant parent and preschool teacher perspectives on English-language acquisition and home-language retention. One of our findings is that most preschool teachers reported having had little or no training in strategies for working with English-language-learning students, and they were largely unaware of the research literature showing the advantages of programs that support the maintenance and development of first-language abilities in young children (Lindholm-Leary and Borsato 2006; MacSwan and Pray 2005; Tse 2001).

Academics

The centrality of play has been long debated in early childhood education, with one side arguing for an emphasis on learning through play and the other for more systematically taught pre-academic skills. The No Child Left Behind Act of 2001, by emphasizing academic readiness and the testing of elementary school students, has had the effect of adding to the pressure on U.S. preschools to emphasize English-language acquisition and early reading instruction for recent immigrants, often at the expense of more play-based curricular approaches (Brown 2009; Kagan and Kauerz 2006; Stipek 2006). A consistent finding of our study is a split—as dramatized in the dialogue that opens this chapter—between the desire of immigrant parents for more emphasis on academic preparation and the argument of their children's teachers that learning and social development should be integrated through a play-based curriculum. In chapter 3, we analyze these differences in the views of contemporary preschool teachers and immigrant parents on the balance of play and academic preparation.

Multiculturalism

Within progressive academic circles, the dominant discourse for working with the young children of recent immigrants is multiculturalism, but multiculturalism is a complex and contentious construct (Darling-Hammond 2007; Fusarelli 2004; Mitakidou et al. 2009). Multicultural education is challenged on one side by Afrocentric and anticolonialist critiques of the fantasy of the nation as a melting pot (Yosso 2002), and on the other side by conservative critiques of multiculturalism as a force that weakens academic standards, balkanizes society into identity groups, and promotes entitlement programs that favor foreign-born over native-born Americans (Horne 2007). In chapter 5, we examine immigrant parent and teacher perspectives on the role of the preschool in helping children develop a sense of citizenship and cultural identity. Most immigrant parents in our study told us they want their children to become "American" but also worry about their children being exposed to negative aspects of American society and losing religious and cultural values. Teachers, while expressing an appreciation for home cultures, often see immigrant parents' adherence to their religious and cultural beliefs as a sign of backwardness and as an obstacle to their children's successful assimilation. Although most of the teachers we interviewed expressed sympathy for the challenges facing the immigrant children they taught and their families, some of their comments reflect the contemporary anti-immigrant sentiments of their communities—and indeed of the country as a whole.

Parental Involvement in Children's Education

Lissak (1983) argues that while Jane Addams was viewed in her time as an advocate for immigrants, Hull House had an uneven record of empowering and being responsive to the wishes of stakeholders in the immigrant communities it served. Lissak draws a distinction between social service programs that give immigrant families what the program believes they need and programs that respond to their clients' wishes. Dory Lightfoot (2004, 100, emphasis in original) argues that this tension continues to characterize many preschool programs:

Despite efforts—which usually seem scrupulous and sincere—to respect parents' wishes and home cultures, programs are generally structured around the assumption that there is one best, or one so-called *normal* path for child development, and that some group of so-called *experts,* such as educational psychologists or program instructors, know better than partici- pating parents how to make children follow this path.

Parental involvement is widely cited as crucial to the educational suc- cess of immigrant children (González, Moll, and Amanti 2005; Gonzalez- Mena 2001, 2008; Hayden, De Goia, and Hadley 2003), but exceedingly difficult to implement effectively (Doucet 2008, 2011a; Vandenbroeck 2009). In chapter 6, we present the perspectives of preschool staff and im- migrant parents on what they see as the problems and possibilities in the relationship between schools and families, and we provide a report on our own not very successful attempt to implement a program aimed at giving immigrant parents greater say about what went on in their children's preschool.

KEY CONCEPTS, FINDINGS, AND RECOMMENDATIONS

In this study, we have employed several innovative concepts—some origi- nal, some adapted from other researchers—to analyze central issues of immigration and early childhood education and to arrive at some implica- tions and recommendations. Among those issues are the need to balance English retention and home-language retention, the (felt) urgency of aca- demic preparation, immigrant children's hybrid identities, the role of bi- cultural/bilingual teachers, and the difficulties in communication be- tween immigrant parents and their children's teachers. The concepts include: parental pragmatism; parents' and teachers' ecological decision- making; the intersectionality of immigration with race, class, and culture; and the false opposition of cultural responsiveness and best practice. We arrive at several implications: that more attention could be paid in teacher education programs to strategies for working with immigrant children and their families; that we need to reconceptualize our notions of best practice and quality in early childhood education to foreground respon- siveness to the diversity of learners, communities, and contexts; that the role played by bilingual/bicultural staff could be better appreciated and supported; and that new models of teacher-parent communication could be developed.

Parental Pragmatism

The tendency of immigrant parents to be pragmatists in their decision-making about their children's early education leads them to choose the necessary over the ideal, based on their felt hierarchy of needs. All parents to some degree are pragmatic, but new immigrant parents are more so, owing to the greater constraints under which they must negotiate life for themselves and their children. The pragmatism of immigrant parents helps to explain, for example, our finding that while almost all of the immigrant parents we interviewed expressed the desire for their children to grow up retaining fluency in their home language, many favored an English-heavy approach over a bilingual one because this desire was trumped by the urgency they felt for their children to quickly acquire fluency in English. For non-immigrant middle-class parents, a bilingual program that gives their child a chance to learn some Spanish or Chinese as a second language is an interesting enrichment option. For new immigrant parents, the risks, on the one hand, of their child failing to become fluent in English before entering elementary school and, on the other, of their child never developing full oral fluency and the ability to read and write in their native language make the stakes of their decisionmaking about language much higher.

This logic also applies to multicultural education: immigrant parents said in our focus groups that passing their cultural and religious values on to their children was a high priority in their parenting, but that it was unrealistic to expect this to be a priority of their children's preschool. Similarly, while many immigrant parents told us that they appreciated the play-based curricular approaches espoused by their children's preschool teachers, their concern about their children being labeled as "behind" when they entered kindergarten led many of them to wish that their children's preschool gave higher priority to academic preparation.

Such pragmatic reasoning led many immigrant parents to conclude that the best solution was a separation of tasks and responsibilities, with the preschool teachers teaching their children English, getting them ready for life in the United States, and preparing them academically for the demands of elementary school, while parents took responsibility for home-language retention, cultural identity, and religious education. Many immigrant parents argued that their children's time in preschool was so precious that attention there needed to be placed on what teachers could give their children that they could not. Thus, as we discuss in chapter 6, many immigrant parents believed that, even if they disagreed with aspects of the preschool's approach, it was better to say nothing and to adopt a deferential stance than to risk losing the goodwill of their children's teachers.

Ecological Decisionmaking

The nuanced positions taken by immigrant parents on questions of language and curriculum reflect not just a general pragmatism and sense of urgency but also a calculation of both the opportunities and the demands of their local setting, leading to what we call "ecological decisionmaking." Considering that new immigrant parents live, work, and send their children to school in highly diverse settings, it is not surprising that the parents in the different locales where we conducted focus groups expressed varying priorities and preferences. Historical gateway cities such as New York and Phoenix present immigrants with different resources and challenges than do cities such as Nashville and small towns such as Riverdale, Iowa, which have much less experience with immigration. Settings where immigrants live in enclaves—speaking their own language with most people they encounter and sharing a cultural background—present different opportunities, but also different challenges, than do settings where immigrants are in the minority in their neighborhoods and schools. These differences in the cultural and linguistic ecology of communities lead immigrants to come to different conclusions about how they want their children's preschool to approach questions of language, culture, academic preparation, and social inclusion.

Immigrant parents take stock not only of what their community and preschool can offer their children but also of their own strengths and weaknesses, as well as their own resources, when it comes to preparing their children for success in school and for life in the United States. Parents who speak limited English look to the preschool to give their children what they cannot give them. Immigrant parents who feel secure in their ability to provide their children with a strong sense of cultural identity and values and who feel confident about their ability to pass on their home language want the preschool to emphasize academic preparation. For these reasons, we suggest that it is necessary to shift the core research question in studies of immigration and education from "What do immigrants need and want from their children's schools?" to "What do immigrants from different backgrounds who settle in different communities that present different challenges and opportunities want and need from their schools?"

Because parents living in different communities want and need different things, we find that we cannot make sweeping conclusions about what immigrant parents expect from their children's preschools. In communities where there are many immigrants from the same cultural and language background, immigrant parents have different concerns about early childhood education than do parents in communities where they are among just a handful of immigrants from their culture. Immigrant parents living in communities that are new to immigration encounter different challenges than do parents living in communities with a long continuous experience of immigration. A parallel argument can be made for teachers, whose thinking about what is most important to teach immigrant children is driven not only by their pedagogical beliefs but also in part by their assessment of the educational and social resources of their community.

To say that immigrant parents tend to be pragmatic and to make decisions based on their assessment of barriers and resources is not to say that these calculations necessarily are correct. New immigrant parents are forced to make crucial decisions about their children's early education based on limited and, in many cases, flawed information (Crosnoe 2007). A lack of fluency in English limits immigrant parents' access to helpful sources of information in their attempts to evaluate risks, resources, and options. Much of the information guiding their decisionmaking is based on stories they have heard from other immigrant parents. They evaluate this information through the prism of their experiences with education in their home country, their folk theories of child-rearing, and the values of their culture of origin.

But to suggest that immigrant parents are inevitably guided by less than perfect information and that they make decisions that may be inconsistent with research findings and recommendations from panels of experts is not to suggest that their perspectives should be discounted or that their calculations are less reasonable or rational than those of their children's teachers or of policymakers, whose decisionmaking about early childhood education also is too often based on inadequate data, misinterpretation or ignorance of the research literature, or political and ideological factors. We need to avoid conceptualizing immigrant parents' perspectives as a form of ignorance while viewing the beliefs of teachers, policymakers, and experts as knowledge.

The Social Conservatism of Immigrant Parents

We can understand immigrant parents' perspectives on early childhood education as reflecting the intersectionality of their status as immigrants, their socioeconomic class, and their cultural, religious, and political beliefs. This suggestion is consistent with Hirokazu Yoshikawa's (2012) study of the child-rearing strategies of undocumented immigrant parents; like our study, Yoshikawa's research reveals the interaction of effects caused by a lack of legal status, poverty, and prejudice, with effects that can be traced to parents' cultural beliefs and experiences back home prior to emigration.

A key finding of our study is that while immigrant parents have some concerns that are specific to being a new immigrant, many of their perspectives align closely with the views of socially conservative Americans. In our focus groups, white and black working-class parents as well as religious middle-class parents raised many of the same concerns raised by new immigrant parents about an emphasis on academic preparation in preschool, children showing respect for teachers and other adults, the acceptability of corporal punishment (Vernon-Feagans 1996), and the importance of protecting children from the hypersexuality of American society. An ironic implication is that some of the demographic groups in the United States most opposed to immigration and to legalizing the status of undocumented immigrants would find these new immigrants, as voters, on their side on many social issues (Fisher 2012). There are signs, however, that the political landscape is changing: some evangelical groups that are conservative on most social issues are beginning to embrace new immigrants as their potential political allies on abortion, gay marriage, and other wedge issues and recruiting them as co-congregants (Lee and Pachon 2007; Taylor, Gershon, and Pantoja 2012; Wong, Rim, and Perez 2008).

The majority of the most comprehensive universal prekindergarten programs in the United States are in the "red" states (NIEER 2011); in 2011 four of the five states with the highest percentage of four-year-olds enrolled in public preschools were Florida, Oklahoma, Georgia, and West Virginia. Although bipartisan support, especially in state legislatures, for increasing the provision of preschool is growing, this does not mean that there are not large ideological differences among supporters about the means and ends of preschool. Debates among scholars about the balance of academics and play in the preschool curriculum reflect in part a deeper ideological schism in American society (Lareau 2003) about fundamental issues: Is knowledge constructed or transmitted? What is the proper authority of teachers and other adults in children's lives? What role do schools play in promoting civic, moral, and religious values?

Immigrants play a complex role in these debates. New immigrants are often identified as one of the sectors of American society most in need of preschools to compensate for perceived parental inadequacies. The strongest advocates for increasing new immigrants' access to early childhood education and care programs and other services tend to be political and social progressives. But if and when their voices are heard, immigrants may become swing voters who side with the more conservative positions on questions of preschool curriculum and pedagogy and other social issues.

The Intersections of Poverty, Prejudice, and Immigration

We were surprised by how much of the time in our focus group discussions was taken up by immigrant parents telling stories, not directly about preschool, but instead about the prejudice they encountered in the larger society and about their economic difficulties. These experiences of prejudicial treatment are rarer for newly arrived middle-class immigrants, suggesting that such prejudice has as much or more to do with social class as with country of origin or immigration status. For example, an immigrant father in a Phoenix focus group told about being treated badly when he stopped after work at a grocery store in a middle-class neighborhood; he ascribed this treatment as much to the fact that he wore dust-covered construction clothes as to his being Mexican and Spanish-speaking: "This time I go to Fry's where the American people go, and I see the difference. They look at me, so clean, and me so dirty, buying chicken. I feel they are staring at me."

A surprising finding is that the parents we interviewed at the preschool of the Phoenix Metro Islamic School, located in Tempe, reported few experiences with prejudice in the wider society. This may be the result in part of the immigration climate in Arizona, where Mexicans are the chief target of anti-immigrant rhetoric and treatment. Had we interviewed parents and teachers at an Islamic school in a community elsewhere in the country that was rife with anti-Muslim rhetoric, it is likely that we would have heard more stories of prejudice. This finding is consistent with the theory that in different communities different groups are the stigmatized "other"—the immigrant group on which anxieties and hostility are most easily projected (Balibar 2003).

In public preschool programs serving children of new immigrants, problems of prejudice and poverty are ever present but daunting for teachers to address. The mission of Head Start and some other public preschool programs is not only to get children off to a good start in life but also to help parents escape from poverty. We were therefore surprised to find that most of the teachers in our focus groups said nothing about their students' poverty or about the racism faced by the students and their families in the larger society. Even when practitioners showed an awareness of the impact of these larger social problems on the families of the children they taught and cared for, they said that they felt at a loss when it came to doing anything about it. When faced with the enormity of these problems, a common response of teachers is to stick to their own area of expertise, which is providing high-quality care and education, and to leave social problems to social workers and social activists.

The Tension Between Cultural Responsiveness and Best Practices

Early childhood practitioners who work with immigrant children often find themselves caught between two core beliefs: on the one hand, they believe in being culturally sensitive and responsive to parents, and on the other, they want to remain faithful to their core professional codes of best practice. Most teachers and directors told us that they support the principle of making their school more welcoming to new immigrants by making accommodations for religious diets, using words from children's home languages in the morning greetings, adding culturally relevant books to the book corner, and celebrating a range of holidays. Most practitioners drew the line, however, at questions of curriculum and pedagogy and were unwilling to accommodate parents' wishes for a more academic approach in preschool. On these questions, they take the position that they "shall not be moved."

To put it another way, the willingness of early childhood educators in our study to be culturally responsive was trumped by their commitment to their notions of best practice, which were centered on the principles of constructivism, learning through play, and resisting a pushed-down academic curriculum. Across the sites in this study we found that preschool teachers were generally reluctant to change the way they relate to parents and to engage with parents in nonhierarchical forms of dialogue. We suggest that practitioners' reluctance to change comes primarily not from any belligerence or lack of concern or empathy, but rather from an understandable hesitation to have their professional practices challenged or compromised. This reluctance is not likely to change without a paradigm shift—that is, not until teachers come to see working collaboratively with parents in general and with immigrant parents in particular as being just as central to their job and their profession as teaching and caring for young children.

Unprepared to Work with New Immigrants

One of the most consistent of our findings across all of the settings is that teachers have had little or no training for the task of working with immigrant children or their parents. Few teachers are prepared to work with English-language learners (ELLs), and because most of them had had little exposure to research on second-language acquisition (Early and Winton 2001), there is widespread overreliance on folk theories such as the notion that learning two languages while still young leads to interlanguage confusion. Except for those who were themselves immigrants, most teachers are unaware of immigrant families' cultural beliefs and practices, contemporary living conditions, and perspectives on early childhood education.

Among the teachers we interviewed, we found a wide range of attitudes, beliefs, and levels of experience. A very few practitioners were openly hostile to immigrant children and families, but many more of the teachers we encountered thought of themselves as supportive and without prejudice toward immigrants; nevertheless, in our focus groups these teachers made statements that were naive, misinformed, unproductive, and potentially offensive. We found considerable variation across sites in teachers' ability to transcend stereotypical and naive views of immigrant children and families. For example, in New York and Phoenix, two urban areas with many immigrants and a long history of immigration, teachers were less likely to speak about immigrants in naive and stereotypical terms than the teachers in Nashville and the small rural town in Iowa, which both had only a recent history of cultural diversity and interaction with immigrants.

These teachers' lack of experience and rhetorical sophistication should not be taken, however, as an indication of a lack of sympathy or an inability to learn to treat immigrant children well or to engage in dialogue with immigrant parents. Beneath statements that suggested naïveté or even anti-immigrant beliefs and sentiments, we detected signs in these teachers of a desire to change and to connect with immigrant children and parents. And behind some of the more sophisticated and politically correct statements of teachers working in New York and Phoenix we sometimes heard sentiments that were less pro-immigrant and inclined to be helpful than they at first seemed.

A clear implication of these findings for policy is that we need pre-service and in-service teacher education programs that include systematic preparation in strategies for working with new immigrant children and their families (Daniel and Friedman 2005; Ray, Bowman, and Robbins 2006). Practitioners must also be given training for working with young English-language learners. Teacher education programs must help practitioners understand that being responsive to immigrant parents' concerns and beliefs, rather than constituting a threat to notions of best practice, is itself a form of best practice.

LISTENING TO THE VOICES OF IMMIGRANT PARENTS

Most preschool programs that serve children of immigrants are hampered by practitioners' and policymakers' lack of knowledge of and consideration for parental perspectives (Carreón, Drake, and Barton 2005; Chrispeels and Rivero 2001; De Gaetano 2007; Doucet 2011a; López 2009; Ramirez 2003; Riojas-Cortez 2001; Rueda and Monzó 2002; Souto-Manning and Swick 2006). The best practices and versions of normative child development that guide early childhood education and care policy are insufficiently informed by culture differences and laden with middle-class, majoritarian values and assumptions (Ballenger 1998; Delpit 1995; Goodwin 2002; Lightfoot 2004; Reese and Gallimore 2000; Vandenbroeck 2009). Immigrant parents' voices introduce perspectives on the social, emotional, cognitive, and academic dimensions of early childhood education that could broaden and challenge dominant notions of best practice (Gonzáles, Moll, and Amanti 2005) and inform policy.

Our study shows that immigrant parents have much to say about what they would like for their children to experience in their preschool programs and much to contribute to discussions of preschool practice and policy. This in itself is an important finding of this study because historically, and to this day, the voices of parents—and particularly those of parents who are recent immigrants—have often been marginalized in debates within preschool programs about preschool policy and practice. We have found that immigrant parents, when given the opportunity to speak about their children's early education, are more often than not passionate, thoughtful, reasonable, and pragmatic.

On the other hand, our study also shows that there are steep barriers that make it difficult for immigrant parents to speak in schools and, when they do, to be heard by educators. These barriers include lack of fluency in a common language between immigrant parents and teachers; customs of deference to teachers and a hesitancy to cause offense or make trouble; and a lack of time, space, and mechanisms for immigrant parents to speak at their children's preschools.

BUILDING BRIDGES BETWEEN SCHOOLS, IMMIGRANT PARENTS, AND IMMIGRANT COMMUNITIES

In the second stage of our study, we attempted to apply the lessons from the research stage to construct new models for teachers and immigrant parents to engage in meaningful dialogue about the means and ends of early childhood education. We used the videos that had served as research tools in the first stage as conversation starters in gatherings we organized of immigrant parents and their children's teachers. While we had some moments of success with these pilot efforts, in most cases we failed. We worked for a year to introduce teachers to concepts such as parents' "Funds of Knowledge" (González, Moll, and Amanti 2005) but failed to significantly change teachers' view of parents as clients needing their instruction to a view of them as educational partners. By the same token, the year we spent trying to cultivate in parents a sense of being equal partners in their children's education, with a meaningful role to play in guiding the preschool's curriculum, mostly failed to shift parents away from their public stance of deference ("agachar") toward teachers.

These experiences have not made us less committed to the value of meaningful dialogue and power-sharing between teachers and immigrant parents, but they have made us more realistic about the hurdles. We find ourselves in agreement with Michel Vandenbroeck's (2009) recent argument that when dialogue is initiated between educators and immigrant communities, things are likely to get worse before they get better, as well as with Fabienne Doucet's (2011a) observation that there are costs as well as benefits to immigrant families of parental involvement in their children's schools. Elsewhere, Doucet (2011b) argues that efforts to build bridges between the worlds of the school and home are resisted by many immigrant parents who fear, not without reason, that such bridges make it possible not only to bring parent perspectives to the school but also to allow the school and the host society to reach further into the life of the family, undermining traditional values and exposing the family to scrutiny and potentially to legal and social service interventions. While pointing out its perils for immigrant families, Doucet acknowledges that bridging the worlds of home and school is worth the effort, if attention is paid to issues of power.

The Te Whariki national early childhood education framework of New Zealand is an example of a curriculum that foregrounds the perspectives of families and communities and calls for "giving effect to a Māori voice within services" (Ritchie and Rau 2008). Maoris, of course, are the indigenous people of New Zealand, not an immigrant group. Nevertheless, there are lessons here for the creation of effective models of immigrant parent participation in their children's education. The Maori case highlights the need to include in the provision of early childhood education services coursework for teachers on bilingualism and on working with students and families from diverse cultural backgrounds, as well as a commitment to curriculum reform that includes the voices of respected members of the communities that schools serve.

Although cultural responsiveness has not historically been a hallmark of U.S. preschool programs serving children of recent immigrants, there are signs of progress. Over the past twenty years, the quality standards of the National Association for the Education of Young Children (NAEYC) have put more and more emphasis on the importance of preschools being culturally as well as developmentally appropriate. The newest Head Start performance standards (Office of Head Start 2009) stress the importance of preparing teachers to understand and be responsive to the needs of immigration families. A recent update to Head Start's *Multicultural Principles for Head Start Programs Serving Children Ages Birth to Five* (Office of Head Start 2008) calls for increasing attention to cultural diversity, developing sensitivity to the needs of English-language learners, and hiring staff who come from the community and cultures served by the program.

The goals and policies set out in these documents are exemplary, but the challenge is in the implementation. There are few data to show to what degree Head Start and other preschool programs are meeting the standards for culturally responsive curricula and nonhierarchical parental involvement. We fear that pressures on Head Start and other publicly funded preschool programs to show that students are meeting standardized assessments goals for English-language learning and academic readiness will work against the implementation of efforts to make preschool programs more culturally responsive. As a recent response by La Raza to the Race to the Top (2011) Early Learning Challenge Grant request for proposals points out:

> Less than a handful of states make any reference to the needs of ELL students, leaving the vast majority of states with no articulated program strategies or policy recommendations to address the needs of ELLs in their state early learning guidelines. The lack of comprehensive early learning standards that address the diverse language and ethnic child populations is alarming. . . . The current QRIS [Quality Rating and Improvement System] systems have been developed with little attention paid to how programs address the needs of culturally and linguistically diverse children and families.

It remains to be seen how calls by the Department of Education and others for uniform standards and assessments will be balanced with attention to the needs and perspectives of immigrant parents and communities.

THE ROLE OF BILINGUAL AND
BICULTURAL STAFF

In our focus group interviews, both immigrant parents and non-immigrant teachers expressed appreciation for bicultural and bilingual staff members—from head teachers to family service coordinators, teacher's aides, and office workers—as sources of information, translators, and mediators. But comments in these interviews also suggested that neither immigrant parents nor non-immigrant teachers appreciated the difficulties faced by bicultural staff members as they struggle to negotiate their in-between position. Teachers who were themselves immigrants discussed both the role they play as cultural and language translators and mediators and the difficulties they encounter in situations where they feel pressured to speak either as the voice of their community or as the voice of the program. Both immigrant parents and non-immigrant school staff look to bicultural and bilingual staff members to provide a bridge between the worlds of home and school (Monzó and Rueda 2008), but both sides tend to underestimate the complexity of this task (Lucero 2010; Rueda, Monzó, and Higareda 2004).

In the course of becoming professionals, immigrant teachers have had to renounce positions they held before joining the field and to adopt its central beliefs—for example, beliefs in play, constructivism, and child-centeredness. On the other hand, immigrant teachers who adopt too completely the positions of their non-immigrant fellow teachers risk being seen as alienated from their culture of origin—or worse, as a traitor to their community.

One policy implication is that we need to recruit and retain more teachers who are recent immigrants. An unfortunate and unintended side effect of the requirement by Head Start and other public preschool programs that all teachers have a four-year college degree and assistant teachers a two-year degree is that many African American, Native American, and bilingual Hispanic teachers and aides lost their jobs in preschools and the profession changed its complexion, becoming more white, Anglo, and middle-class. Recruiting more people who are bilingual and bicultural into the field of early childhood education requires effort on several fronts: for instance, programs that allow teacher's aides and part-time staff to complete two-year and four-year certification programs while retaining their jobs must be created and funded, and community colleges and universities must ramp up their efforts to attract bilingual and bicultural candidates into early childhood education programs.

Another policy implication is that we must acknowledge the value of bilingual and bicultural staff to pre-service and in-service teacher education programs, as well as the difficulties these staff members face in balancing their responsiveness to the school and to their community.

THE VALUE OF PRESCHOOL TO IMMIGRANT CHILDREN AND FAMILIES

Our focus on areas of difference in the perspectives of immigrant parents and their children's teachers should not obscure the fact that the great majority of the immigrant parents in our study expressed appreciation for the opportunity to send their children to preschool. Critical comments made by parents were often introduced with such phrases as, "I really like the teachers here," or, "I am grateful my child is able to attend this school." Even if they wanted some adjustments made to the program, none of the parents told us that they did not value their child's preschool experience.

Our informants' general sense of appreciation for the value of their children's preschool experience is consistent with the research literature, all of which shows academic gains (McCartney 2004; Reynolds 2003) and long-term economic advantages (Masse and Barnett 2002; Nores et al. 2005; Schweinhart et al. 1993) for children who attend high-quality early childhood programs (Myers 2005). Studies show that prekindergarten programs are particularly beneficial for immigrant, English-language-learning children, especially when staff for these programs are bilingual and have some training in working with ELL students (Garcia 2007).

The policy implications here are complex. Many states have recently implemented versions of universal prekindergarten programs. But with funding for these programs limited, there are intense policy debates about whether all children under age five should be enrolled in them or whether they should be targeted at children seen as being at risk because they do not speak English, are poor, or have been identified as having special needs. In many states and localities, as at the national level, there are debates about the ratio of funds that go for prekindergarten programs versus all-day kindergarten; for programs for children in the year or two before they enter kindergarten versus programs for children from birth to age three; and for programs that focus more narrowly on children's academic and social development versus more comprehensive programs that include a focus on health, social services, and parental education (Fuller 2007; Tobin, Hsueh, and Karasawa 2009).

While our findings cannot resolve these tensions, they do allow us to present immigrant parents' perspectives on these policy questions. Most of the immigrant parents in our focus groups expressed a preference for family arrangements for child care for children under age three rather than center-based child care. Most said that they valued a year or two of preschool to get their children ready for kindergarten. Most wanted the program to stress English-language acquisition, learning the routines of school, and academic readiness. All of the parents wanted their children's preschools to have staff members who knew their language and had respect for their culture.

PRESCHOOLS AS CRUCIBLES FOR THE CREATION OF NEW CITIZENS

Although our study clearly shows that there are often large gaps between the perspectives of immigrant parents and teachers, and that efforts to create, implement, and sustain dialogue and negotiation face formidable obstacles, we also found considerable goodwill on both sides and a sense of empowerment for teachers as well as parents in the moments when real dialogue between them has occurred.

Although there are risks to this venture, the risk of doing nothing is higher. What is at stake here is more than just improving early childhood education and care services for immigrant children and their families. In the contemporary world, preschools are the most salient sites where the immigrant's culture of home meets the culture of the host society. As such, preschools that serve immigrant children and their families are crucibles for the creation of new citizens, new communities, and hybrid social and cultural forms.

In the first great era of immigration in the United States in the early years of the twentieth century, settlement house preschools were charged with the mission of creating American citizens out of immigrant children. Most of these programs followed an assimilationist paradigm in which there was little respect for immigrant parents, scant interest in maintaining the heritage languages and cultural identities of immigrant children, and little appreciation for the contributions that new immigrants could (and inevitably would) make to the transformation of the host culture and society. Now, a century later, in another great period of immigration, preschools can play a new role—as sites not only for young children to become members of the new society, but for them and their families to join with preschool teachers and directors in a process of cultural and social construction.

Chapter 2 | Community Contexts and Research Methods

IN THE UNITED STATES, as of 2010, there were 8.7 million children under age eight with at least one foreign-born parent, a number that had doubled since 1990 (Fortuny, Hernandez, and Chaudry 2010). Immigrant families from Mexico, South America, and Central America make up 63 percent of the total immigrant population (Fortuny, Hernandez, and Chaudry 2010). Latino children of immigrants are the fastest-growing group of students attending early childhood education programs around the country (Garcia 2007). But the percentage of Americans who were born in another country is just part of the story. Because immigrant parents tend to be younger and to have more children than their U.S.-born peers, the percentage of immigrant children in preschools is much higher than the percentage of immigrants in the overall population (Fortuny, Hernandez, and Chaudry 2010). Thus, in cities such as Los Angeles, Chicago, and Phoenix a majority of the children attending public preschools come from Spanish-speaking homes. This is also the case in some rural communities, such as the small city in Iowa that we call "Riverdale," which served as one of the field sites for this study; over half of the children attending preschool in Riverdale spoke Spanish at home. For California as a whole, in 2012, 73 percent of children enrolled in Head Start were Hispanic or Latino, and over 50 percent of the total Head Start enrollment came from Spanish-speaking homes. Because Spanish-speaking immigrants from Mexico and Central America are the largest and fastest-growing segment of the preschool population, in this study we focus mostly but not exclusively on preschools in communities with significant numbers of Spanish-speakers.

Because the United States lacks a national system of early childhood education and care, the educational experiences of young children are highly diverse. About 30 percent of children under age five are cared for at home, and relatives look after another 10 percent. Nonparental care options include care by relatives, care by nonkin in family home-care settings, and care in center-based programs, such as Head Start and private nonprofit and for-profit preschools. Attendance in programs of various types is highly correlated with immigration status and culture of origin (Fuller 2007). Of the immigrant children who attend center-based programs, a higher percentage are enrolled in Head Start than is true for native-born children, who are more likely to attend private preschools (Garcia 2007).

Although in theory the diversity of early childhood education and care possibilities available in the United States would seem to give immigrant parents many choices, in reality these choices are heavily constrained. Hispanic parents enroll their children in preschools at a lower percentage than white and black parents, but it is unclear how much of this gap is due to a preference for home care by relatives and how much to a lack of information and access (Garcia 2007).

Private preschool programs are prohibitively expensive for most immigrant parents. New immigrants from Mexico and other countries tend to lack knowledge about the formal child care market (Crosnoe 2007), and most communities with a high percentage of new immigrants have few if any accredited preschool programs other than those run by Head Start and school districts (Fuller 2007; Loeb et al. 2004).

Our focus in this study is on the types of center-based early childhood education and care programs that most typically serve the children of recent immigrants; most of these programs are supported by federal and state tax dollars, are often run in conjunction with elementary schools, and offer free or deeply reduced tuition to income-qualifying families. They offer one year or two years of half-day or full-day preschool to children three to five years old. About half of the sites where we conducted interviews were Head Start programs; among the other half, programs were run and supported with block grant and other state funds. We did not interview immigrant parents whose children were cared for by relatives in non-center-based care arrangements, whose children attended child care programs for children under age three, or whose children attended private preschools (the exceptions being the parents we interviewed at the private Islamic school in the greater Phoenix area).

THE EFFECTS OF COMMUNITY CONTEXT

Excellent qualitative studies of aspects of immigration and early childhood education and care have been conducted in single sites. For example, Guadalupe Valdez (1996) conducted a case study of ten first-generation Mexican immigrant families' views on educating their young children near the Texas-Mexico border in a community she called Las Fuentes. Cynthia Ballenger (1998) conducted her study of Haitian immigrant parents' feelings about their children's preschool experience in a single Head Start center in Boston. Claude Goldenberg, Ronald Gallimore, Leslie Reese, and Helen Garnier (2001) studied the educational expectations and aspirations of Latino parents for their young children in two communities in Los Angeles. Concha Delgado-Gaitan and Henry Trueba (1991) explored Hispanic child-rearing in an unnamed community in northern California. All of the immigrant families in Hirokazu Yoshikawa's (2012) study of the child-rearing strategies of recent immigrants from Mexico, the Dominican Republic, and China lived in New York City. Although we would expect that much of what these researchers found in their studies would be true as well for immigrants from these cultures living in other U.S. settings, there is also reason to expect variation by location, as Alejandro Portes and Min Zhou (1993), among others, have suggested.

Nancy Foner's (2005, 34) reflections on the value of historical comparative research on immigration applies as well to multi-sited comparative work: "A comparative approach undermines two contrary but equally damaging presuppositions—the illusion of total regularity and the illusion of absolute uniqueness. In other words, it enables us to see what is unique to a specific situation and what is more general to the migration experience." To assess the impact of location on the experiences of immigrant children and parents and parents' decisions about early childhood education therefore requires a multi-sited research approach. Bruce Fuller (2007, 258) rightly praises studies such as those of Angela Valenzuela and Sanford Dornbusch (1994), Lucinda Pease-Alvarez (2002), and Leslie Reese and Ronald Gallimore (2000) for employing an ecological framework that:

> sees Latino families as situated in highly variable local communities, from deeply impoverished immigrant areas to blue-collar suburbs that ring urban centers. The developmental niches that emerge for young children are viewed as open systems. That is, parents must adapt their child rearing practices, from keeping toddlers inside to avoid danger, to accommodating job and childcare options that arise in the environment. Persisting, resilient cultural models and norms may add to the family's cohesion, but the ecological perspective emphasizes that the inability to adapt to new economic and social surroundings can limit opportunity for parent and child alike.

Not all studies of immigration and early childhood education are based on research in a single location. Fuller's own *Standardized Childhoods* (2007) is more about the battle over universal prekindergarten programs than it is about immigration and early childhood education, but this book demonstrates the virtue of a contrastive approach to analyses of how early childhood education and care issues play out in settings as dissimilar as California and Oklahoma, as well as analyses of prekindergarten programs serving immigrants in the Bay Area and Los Angeles. The report of the National Taskforce for the Early Education of Hispanics (Garcia 2007) provides a nationwide analysis of the problem of Hispanic educational underachievement. This report is based on an analysis of large data sets—such as the National Institute of Child Health and Human Development (NICHD) Study of Early Child Care and Youth Development, the 2000 census, and achievement test data—rather than on a multi-sited research design or an analysis aimed at highlighting differences between locations. Robert Crosnoe's (2007) analysis of the effects of attending preschool on Mexican immigrant children's academic achievement is a good example of a study that draws on NICHD data to make nuanced conclusions that take location into account.

Our multi-sited approach fits into the gap between the single-sited ethnographic studies and the large-data-set nationwide studies and is conceptually consistent with Portes and Zhou's (1993) theory of segmented assimilation, which emphasizes the need to disaggregate immigrant experience. Emphasizing the impact of the contexts where new immigrants live, Portes and Zhou suggest that there are differential outcomes for children of new immigrants who live in communities where they are drawn into oppositional subcultures of native-born citizens and children of new immigrants who are largely immersed in a coethnic community. Our method of conducting interviews in a variety of settings across the country allows us to explore such contrasting impacts of context, including: the size, homogeneity, and social and political concerns of the receiving community; whether immigrants in the preschool come from mostly one country or from many countries; the presence or absence of native-born children in the preschool; and the presence or absence of a native-born immigrant community, including, importantly, the presence or absence in the preschool of staff who share a language and cultural background with the new immigrant families.

THE RESEARCH METHOD

The method of this study is video-cued multivocal ethnography. This is the method used by Joseph Tobin in collaboration with David Wu and Dana Davidson in *Preschools in Three Cultures: Japan, China, and the United States* (1989) and also with Yeh Hsueh and Mayumi Karasawa in the sequel, *Preschool in Three Cultures Revisited* (2009). As in those studies, we made a videotape of a typical day in a classroom for four-year-olds in a U.S. preschool and then used this videotape as a tool to stimulate a multi-vocal, intercultural dialogue. Our research partners in Europe also made videos of typical days in preschools in their countries, and we used these European videos as additional interviewing cues for our interviews in the United States with parents and teachers.

In this method of video-cued multivocal ethnography, the videotapes function primarily not as data but rather as a cue or stimulus, like a set of interview questions in conventional social science research. The core assumption of the method is that the video material we shoot and edit is a stimulus that is richer, better contextualized, and less abstract than a verbal question asked in an interview. Being able to comment on scenes in a video is a more concrete, less daunting task for parents and teachers than being asked to answer abstract questions about preschool pedagogical and curricular practices. It is tough to answer the question "How do you believe teachers should deal with conflicts in the classroom?" but much easier to comment on a scene in a video that shows a teacher dealing in a certain way with a playground altercation. By providing a common object for attention, the videos in our study served to create a sense of community and shared purpose in the focus group interviews, thus facilitating conversation among people who had often come to the meeting not knowing each other.

The other key feature of this method is the production of a multivocal conversation among parents, teachers, and directors across disparate settings in which all were talking about the same video. As in a projective test, the differences in how people responded to our tapes reveal differences in their beliefs and worldviews. As we showed a video made in a classroom to the classroom practitioner, then to her colleagues, the parents of the children she cared for, and the audiences of parents and teachers at other preschool sites across the country, we created a virtual conversation among a diverse community of stakeholders.

The video-cued method inevitably raises questions of typicality: how can we claim that one preschool setting was typical of the country, or that the day we videotaped was typical of other days in that preschool? We were able to address the typicality of the day we videotaped by beginning our investigation with questions for the teachers at the preschool we videotaped: Did our tape show a typical day? If not, in what ways was it atypical? By showing a tape made in one setting to audiences in many other settings, we enlisted our informants in the task of helping us understand in what ways the site we chose was typical and in what ways it reflected regional, ideological, or programmatic variations within the country.

The Video Cue

We shot a video of a more or less typical day in the morning class for four-year-olds at Solano Preschool—a public preschool located in and run by the Phoenix Elementary School District—from the time when the children arrived to the time of their departure. We used two video cameras, each connected to a camera-mounted microphone and a wireless mic worn by one of the teachers. The day after filming we showed the classroom teachers the footage we shot in their classroom, fast-forwarding to key moments and asking about the context of the events captured in our footage and the thinking behind their actions. Based on the initial feedback from the teachers, we edited the eight hours of videotape down to twenty minutes. The logic of this winnowing process was to select a balance of shots that best reflected the program's approach to working with children of immigrants and shots that we anticipated would function effectively as cues to stimulate informants to explicate their beliefs and philosophies. After showing the edited video to the classroom teachers and the preschool director to make sure they were comfortable with its content, we then made additional edits, as needed.

Solano Preschool was supported by state block grant funding. (The program was eliminated in 2011 because of a loss of funding.) Children qualified for the tuition-free program if they came from a family earning less than 125 percent of the poverty line or if the primary language spoken at home was not English. Children attended five days a week for two and a half hours each day, in either the morning or afternoon class.

The year we filmed at Solano, about half of the twelve students in the class we videotaped were children of recent immigrants who came from Spanish-speaking homes. The other children in the class included three Hispanic children from second- and third-generation immigrant families, an African American child, a Native American child, and two recent non-Mexican immigrant children, one from Vietnam and one from Bosnia. A teacher at Solano estimated that 90 percent of the recently arrived Mexican immigrant families with children in the program were undocumented. Elodia "Lolie" Gomez, the teacher in the class we filmed, emigrated from Mexico as a teenager, and the assistant teacher, Aczelia Enriquez, emigrated from Guatemala as a young adult. Both switched back and forth throughout the school day from English to Spanish in their interactions with the children and with parents.

Solano's administrators described their NAEYC-accredited program as child-centered and play-based. We would describe their curricular approach as eclectic: periods of free play, recess, and student-selected activity centers alternated with teacher-led activities, including a calendar-based morning opening, songs, and a story. Learning centers included art, language arts, mathematics, science, and dramatic play. On some days the head teacher led an activity that involved one or more of these content areas. Although there was no formal bilingual approach guiding the program, both teachers and many of the children code-switched between English and Spanish throughout the day.

The "Day at Solano Preschool" video opens with Lolie unlocking the door of the portable building that houses her classroom, entering, and setting up materials for the day. As parents and grandparents sign in their children, Lolie, Aczelia, and the school's social worker, Roberta Figueroa (who spends one a day a week in Lolie's classroom), chat with the parents in both Spanish and English. Lolie takes Michael, who is crying and having a hard time separating from his mother, in her lap and comforts him. During the free-play period that follows, we see Marie, a Vietnamese girl who is learning English, engage in an argument in the dramatic play area about a fancy dress with Elena, then Lolie coming over to mediate the dispute. The teachers move around the classroom during free play, interacting with the children in English and Spanish. During circle time, Lolie reads a book to the class in English, adding brief Spanish translation and asking follow-up questions in both languages. Circle time is followed by a trip to the playground; an activity in which the children draw pictures about the story Lolie has read them; more free play; and finally a second circle time, with dancing and songs. At the end of the day, Lolie hugs each child good-bye and greets and chats with parents in English and Spanish.

The Focus Group Interviews

The first focus group we conducted was with the parents of the children in the video. We showed them the video and then moderated a discussion in English and Spanish. The next focus group was with Solano staff (the director, social worker, and teachers and assistant teachers). The next step was to use the Solano video as a cue for focus group interviews with teachers and parents at preschools in other neighborhoods in and around Phoenix, in Nuevo Campo, Arizona, in Nashville, in Riverdale, Iowa, and in two neighborhoods of New York City. In each of these communities, we had separate discussions with parents and with teachers.

In some of these settings, all or most of the parents were recent immigrants. Some of the settings served a mixture of recent immigrants and non-immigrants. We did not conduct research in any settings where a majority of the children in the program were not children of recent immigrants. Some sites where we conducted research, like the Head Start program in Harlem, served a mixture of immigrant and native-born families, but only the immigrant parents attended our focus group sessions. In

Riverdale, Iowa, where almost half of the students came from Anglo, non-immigrant families, we conducted separate focus groups in Spanish with immigrant parents and ones in English with non-immigrant parents. Because the focus of our study is on the perspectives of immigrant parents, we have not included analyses of the focus groups with non-immigrant parents. In a few of the sites, the focus groups included a mixture of more recent immigrants and those who arrived earlier. When we present examples from these heterogeneous groups, we indicate, when we know, how long the speakers had been in the country.

We organized the screenings with parents in various ways. In some settings, mothers who did not work outside the home were invited to watch and discuss the tapes over coffee and snacks after they dropped their children off in the classroom. In other settings, mothers, fathers, and other family members were invited to screenings of the videotapes in the evenings and on weekends. In some settings, we organized homogeneous groups of parents who spoke the same language and came from similar cultural backgrounds. These group discussions were conducted in the parents' native language and facilitated whenever possible by a researcher who was a member of their community. At some sites, we ran heterogeneous focus groups in which immigrant parents from a variety of cultural and language backgrounds engaged with each other and with non-immigrant parents in discussions about their children's preschool.

Recently arrived immigrant parents spoke most easily and eloquently in focus groups we organized that were homogeneous (all of the parents were from the same cultural backgrounds), where the discussion was conducted in their first language, and where the interviewer was a member of their culture. For example, in focus groups conducted with Mexican mothers by a Latina interviewer, in Spanish, the barriers to speaking and being heard were much lower than in focus groups that included immigrant parents who were from several different countries or did not speak a common language and in focus groups conducted in the language of the host country, by an interviewer who was not an immigrant.

From the point of view of social science methodology, it would have been desirable to have less variety in the way the focus group sessions were conducted. But in doing research in local early childhood education and care settings, we held to the belief that it is more important to adjust to local wishes, needs, and conditions than to attempt to impose methodological rigidity. Moreover, our focus group interview sessions were not just a way of conducting research—they were also meaningful community events for the participating preschool programs. For example, after we invited all of the parents with children in the preschool to attend the focus group session in Riverdale, a town of two thousand people, sixty parents showed up. Rather than turn anyone away, we divided the parents into six focus groups and recruited colleagues from the University of Iowa (Gail Boldt and Karen Wohlwend) to facilitate. The evening program, which included a dinner we provided that brought together the Anglo and Mexican communities, was a significant intercultural event for this small town. Group size, use of interpreters, and the homogeneity of the groups varied accordingly.

In each setting, we began the discussions by asking for reactions to the videotapes. We then asked follow-up questions, both about the videotape and about issues not shown in the videos that were raised by focus group participants. Follow-up questions included: "What do you think about the balance of play and academics (like learning the ABCs) in the video?" "How do you think preschools should deal with teaching English?" "What about helping to maintain home languages?" "What did you think about the Pledge of Allegiance scene in the video?" "Do you think of your child as American? As Mexican? As Mexican American?"

In the focus group sessions, when time permitted, in addition to showing parents and teachers the twenty-minute Solano Preschool videotape, we showed videotapes that had been shot for the larger project in preschools in Italy and France. Parent and teacher comments on what they found attractive or repugnant in the practices of other countries served to clarify and highlight their own beliefs and values. For example, many immigrant parents were impressed with the school-like atmosphere they saw in the video of the French preschool, as well as critical of the French teachers' lack of supervision of the children on the playground. Teachers, in contrast, were critical of what they perceived to be a lack of developmentally appropriate practice by the French teachers and praised the play orientation and constructivism they saw in the Italian preschool video.

About half of the participants in our teacher focus groups were head teachers, and half were assistant teachers and teacher's aides (see table 2.1). Most of the head teachers had a bachelor's (four-year) degree, and most of the assistant teachers had an associate (two-year) degree, with certification in early childhood education. The exceptions were teachers who were working toward these degrees, which at the time of our research were increasingly required in accredited programs.

A limitation of this study is that we did not systematically interview preschool directors, social workers, and other family support staff. In a few of our settings, directors and family service coordinators participated in the teacher focus groups, and in a few we also had the chance to interview administrators—like the director of the New York Head Start program quoted at the beginning of chapter 1, who was disinclined to accede to the wish of some immigrant parents to make the curriculum more explicitly academic. If we had conducted more interviews with directors and family service coordinators, we could have presented a more comprehen-

Table 2.1 Focus Group Interviews with Staff: School/Participant Characteristics

City	School	Type	Gender	Participants	Teachers' Origins
Phoenix	Solano	State	Female	4	Mexico, Guatemala
	King Waters	Head Start	Female	4	Mexico
	Islamic School	Private, religious	1 male	7	Scotland, Morocco, Albania, Iraq
	Nuevo Campo[a]	Head Start	Female	3	Mexico
Nashville	Antioch	Private, religious	Female	5	White and African American
	Franklin[c]	Private, religious[b]	Female	5	African American
	Oak	Private, religious		4	White American
New York City	Harlem	Head Start	1 male 5 female	6	Nigeria, Ivory Coast, Sierra Leone
	Garden Grove[a]	Head Start	1 male 8 female	9	Dominican Republic, Mexico
Riverdale	Riverdale	State	Female	7	White American
Total	9 school sites	6 public 3 private		54	

Source: Authors' fieldwork.
[a]Conducted in Spanish.
[b]Free tuition.

sive portrait of how preschools conceptualize and implement the range of services they provide to immigrant children and families.

We conducted, transcribed, translated (when needed), and coded a total of twenty-seven focus group interviews with parents and sixteen with teachers (see table 2.2). In addition to English and Spanish, we conducted focus groups with parents in Somali and Arabic. The quotes from parents we present in this book are taken from the English translations of these interviews.

Data Analysis

We employed two parallel modes of analysis: content analysis tied to our coding categories and interpretive/textual analysis, which borrowed analytic techniques from structural anthropology, discourse analysis, and Bakhtinian literary analysis (Bakhtin 1990; Tobin 2000). The content analysis allowed us to access and manipulate the data more efficiently and effectively, as well as to make the archive of the focus group interviews more useful in the future to other researchers. The interpretive analysis allowed us to find deeper meanings in the transcripts.

We developed our coding categories based on our review of the literature on immigration and early childhood education and on codes that emerged from our reflections on the interviews (Adair and Pastori 2011). We ended up with codes and subcodes in the areas of curriculum, language, identity, culture, experiences of prejudice and poverty, parent-school interaction, parenting, and the purposes of preschool.

THE RESEARCH SETTINGS

We selected the communities where we conducted focus groups to capture a wide range of the demographic and sociopolitical contexts in which recent immigrants live, work, and send their children to school. These settings include Phoenix (where, as political debates rage, about half of the children in the public schools are children of immigrants, the great majority from Mexico and Central America); New York (a traditional gateway city where recent arrivals from Mexico and Central America are a rising percentage of the immigrant population); Nashville (a historically white and black city with a growing Hispanic population); Riverdale, Iowa, a town of two thousand residents that has become about half Mexican in the past decade); and Nuevo Campo, a town of fifteen thousand mostly Spanish-speakers on the Arizona/Sonora border. (Again, Riverdale and Nuevo Campo are pseudonyms.)

Phoenix is a city that from its beginning has been a diverse and con-

Table 2.2 Focus Group Interviews with Parents: School/Participant Characteristics

City	School	Type	Focus Groups	Gender	Total	Immigrant Communities Represented by Parents
	Solano	State	4	21 mothers, 13 fathers	34	Mexico, Vietnam, Iran, Iraq
	King Waters	Head Start	3	15 mothers, 7 fathers	22	Mexico, indigenous Mexico (Mixtec)
Phoenix	Islamic School	Private, religious	2	9 mothers, 4 fathers	13	Kenya, Jordan, Somalia, Pakistan, Turkey, Egypt, Lebanon, Palestine
	Nuevo Campo	Head Start	1	10 mothers, 1 grandfather	11	Mexico
	Taft	State	4	26 mothers	26	Mexico, Ethiopia
	Jefferson	State	2	10 mothers	10	Mexico, Colombia
Nashville	University	Head Start	1	6 mothers	6	Mexico, Guatemala
	Antioch	Private, religious[a]	1	9 mothers	9	Mexico
	Franklin	Private, religious[a]	1	11 mothers	11	Mexico
New York City	Parker	Head Start	2	8 mothers, 5 fathers	13	Honduras, Yemen, Ivory Coast, Jamaica, Dominican Republic, Sudan, Mali, Senegal
	Monroe	Head Start	2	14 mothers, 3 fathers	17	Dominican Republic, Mexico, Argentina
Riverdale	Riverdale	State	4	19 mothers, 8 fathers	27	Mexico, El Salvador
Iowa City	Lee	Community center	2	14 mothers	14	Somali; Mexican
Total	11 school sites		29	172 mothers, 41 fathers	213	

Source: Authors' fieldwork.
[a]No tuition.

tested place. During the years we conducted our research, Arizona became the epicenter for American immigration tensions, with a sheriff notorious for his roundups of immigrants and a state legislature determined to pass anti-immigration legislation. Phoenix is home to many new immigrants not only from Mexico but also from Africa, eastern Europe, southern Asia, and the Middle East. Phoenix has a long-established Mexican American community and many bilingual and bicultural early childhood educators. We conducted focus groups not only in central Phoenix but also in the surrounding semi-urban communities of Mesa and Tempe and the rural-turning-suburban community of Queen Creek. At Solano, the central Phoenix preschool where we shot the stimulus video and conducted focus groups, about two-thirds of the students were children of recent immigrants, the majority of whom had come from rural communities in Sonora, Mexico. Most of the participants in our parent focus groups in Mesa were recent immigrants from Mexico and Central America. Because enrollment in these state block grant programs is income-based, all of the families were low-income. Most of the parents we interviewed in Queen Creek were Mixtec-speakers from several nearby villages in Oaxaca, Mexico; many of them were not fluent in Spanish. The Phoenix Metro Islamic School in Tempe was the most diverse of our research settings in terms of the number of countries of origin and home languages represented and the range of socioeconomic status among the students. The parent groups we conducted there included a Lebanese engineer, an Egyptian businessman and his wife, a Somali taxi driver, Pakistani housewives, and graduate students and their wives from Jordan and Bosnia.

Nuevo Campo is on the U.S. side of the border between Sonora, Mexico, and Arizona. Of its population of fifteen thousand, 98.7 percent are of Mexican descent, almost all from the state of Sonora. Although English is the official language of government and instruction in Nuevo Campo, much of public daily life is conducted in Spanish and a majority of families speak Spanish at home.

New York City, with a long and famous history of immigration, is increasingly home to new immigrants from Mexico and Central America (Smith 2005). Hispanic New York also includes long-established Puerto Rican and Dominican communities. We conducted focus groups in two New York settings: one a neighborhood on the Upper West Side, the other in Harlem. The Upper West Side setting is home to both an older Dominican community and new arrivals from Mexico and Central America. The Harlem preschool where we conducted focus groups serves children of new immigrants from West Africa (Senegal, Ivory Coast, and Mali) and the West Indies, as well as African American children.

Until recently a city that was mostly black and white, Nashville in the last decade has become the home of many more immigrants, mostly from Mexico and Central America. The city is now approximately 60 percent white, 30 percent black, and 10 percent Hispanic. We conducted focus groups in Nashville at a Head Start center that serves a mixture of Mexican and Central American immigrant families and African American families; at two church-based preschools that serve Mexican-heritage and Central American immigrant families; and at a private Christian preschool that serves Asian immigrant families and white native families.

Riverdale, Iowa, is a small rural town that until recently was almost all Anglo-white; now, thanks to the opening of a meatpacking plant, about half of its population is made up of recent immigrants, mostly from rural communities in Mexico. Population decline in many of the surrounding small towns has led to the closing and consolidation of schools and the shuttering of businesses, but the influx of new immigrants has allowed Riverdale to keep its elementary school open and its main street mostly occupied. In Iowa we also conducted interviews with low-income immigrant parents from Sudan, Mexico, and Central America at two community centers in Iowa City.

The sites where we conducted focus group interviews with teachers and parents include Head Start programs, state prekindergarten programs attached to elementary schools, and one private program. There are a variety of reasons why we would predict that these types of programs would have different curricular approaches and produce different outcomes in children. Head Start and state prekindergarten programs have different core missions, serve overlapping but different populations, and have different training requirements and reward structures. However, as Janelle Wong, Kathy Rim, and Haven Perez (2008, 150) observe, comparing Head Start and state programs is challenging:

The problem with such blanket comparisons is that there is also great variation among state programs, among Head Start programs, and within programs in the same state or region. A difference also exists in the emphasis given to cognitive achievement gains. They are included among Head Start's goals and are becoming ever more central to that program. But Head Start emphasizes health and nutrition programming, parental education and involvement, and coordination with social services. Four of the five states in our sample set comprehensive standards for physical well-being and social and emotional development, but they varied in their provisions around vision, hearing, and health screenings; referrals to social service; meals and snacks; and parental education. While we know how well Head Start did in noncognitive areas—nearly all coefficients are positive but quite small and rarely reliable—we do not know how well the state programs did in these non-tested areas.

Within our research sites, we see as much variation among the Head Start programs and among the state programs as between Head Start and state programs. For example, Monroe, the Head Start program on the Upper West Side of Manhattan, is geographically and philosophically close to the Bank Street College, one of the meccas for constructivist early childhood education. The director and some staff at Monroe have degrees from Bank Street and in our interviews cited Bank Street's influence on their practice. In contrast, the Queen Creek Head Start program is a partnership between Head Start and Chicanos Por La Causa, a nonprofit organization that focuses on Mexican immigrant educational concerns. It is not surprising that we found more emphasis on constructivist play at Monroe and more emphasis on cultural responsiveness at Queen Creek. And while state prekindergarten programs tend to require more years of training than do Head Start programs, the gap is narrowing. In our study, region seemed to play a greater role than program type: the teachers in the two New York City Head Start programs had more years of education than did their Head Start and state prekindergarten counterparts in Arizona.

Other factors that cut across Head Start and state programs include the presence or absence of staff who are themselves immigrants and bilingual and the teachers' years of experience and degrees. As Diane Early and her colleagues (Early, Bryant et al. 2006; Early, Maxwell et al. 2007) and Robert Pianta and his colleagues (2009) have shown, there is no simple correlation between program type, teachers' educational attainment, and program quality. Intervening variables include the type and recency of the educational experience and the teacher hiring and retention dynamics of the particular program. For example, in a program attached to an elementary school, the strongest teachers may be moved from preschool classrooms to the elementary grades, leaving behind teachers who are not as strong (Early et al. 2007, 575). Teachers' warmth and consistency may have as much to do with how well their students do as their years of training, if not more. Indeed, this was the clear message of the immigrant parents who told us that what they most valued was a teacher who cared about their child.

Our qualitative, multi-site research method allows us to reflect on the interaction between program type and community context and leads us to suggest that a program's curricular approach has as much to do with teachers' assessment of the opportunities and constraints of life in their local community as their university coursework or national and state directives, policies, and guidelines—and may in fact be even more influential.

Chapter 3 | Curriculum

MANY OF THE IMMIGRANT PARENTS in our focus groups expressed appreciation for the quality of the toys and play opportunities available to their children in a U.S. preschool, some noting that the early childhood education settings in their home country often lacked such resources. As an immigrant mother from Guatemala said in a focus group in New York City, "Back home, there was nothing to play with in the classroom. Not like here. No toys or paints." Nevertheless, in spite of their appreciation for the way a play-oriented curriculum created a welcoming atmosphere for their children, in our focus groups the great majority of immigrant parents expressed a concern that the curriculum was unbalanced, with insufficient emphasis on academics. For example, Mexican mothers in a focus group in Mesa, Arizona, made these comments on the video they had just watched of a day at Solano Preschool:

MOTHER 1: I liked the bilingual teaching they had. However, it seemed to be that it was low academically.

MOTHER 2: It was all about playing. All.

MOTHER 1: I would say, most of all it was about singing.

MOTHER 3: Well, yes. But they are little. First they have to understand little by little, don't they? Like my child. With him, play comes first. He knows some things, but not at the level of being at school, where he's learning now. He knows his name, he writes it and all that.

MOTHER 4: I think that there has to be a balance.

INTERVIEWER: A balance between what?

MOTHER 4: Between education and play, equal parts I would say.

MOTHER 1: I would say maybe something like 20 percent more education.

MOTHER 2: Yes, it seems that it's not balanced. I think that everything has to have some percentage of balance, because just playing is not okay. There's a purpose to send them to school, right?

In some of these discussions, parents expressed a sense of loss for the more academic kind of preschool program their children would have been experiencing had the family not emigrated to the United States. For instance, a Mexican father in Phoenix said:

FATHER: In my opinion, the school in Mexico is better.

INTERVIEWER: The school is better? How so?

FATHER: Because a child there, he can do multiplication like this [*pointing to his forehead*], using his mind. And here they don't.

A Sudanese mother in Iowa City made similar comments:

> In my country in Sudan, the system is towards the child has to learn to read and write and academics more than anything. ABCs and like things like that. It's not like [there's] a wide variety of things to do. But it's still, the child is free, like in a way the French children in the video, they go out on the playground and play, and they come back in and work.

This mother was commenting favorably here on the video she had just watched of a day in the school in Paris. The video showed children doing writing worksheets, which were checked by the teacher, and then going out on the playground, where they played freely, even wildly, with little adult mediation, in contrast to the U.S. video, which showed teachers doing more supervision of children's play, both indoors and on the playground.

In each focus group we asked: "What do you think about the balance in the video you just watched between play and reading and mathematics?" Some parents liked the balance of play and academics in the Solano video; the great majority said that they would have liked to see the balance tipped more toward academics; no one said that they would have liked to see more play and less academics. This perspective, as we show later in the chapter, is in stark contrast to that of the American teachers who watched the same video and responded to this question by criticizing the Solano Preschool for not having more unstructured play and fewer teacher-led activities.

Most immigrant parents answered our question about balance with explicit requests for more academics, as in this discussion with a group of parents at the Islamic School in Tempe:

INTERVIEWER: What do you want? What's the right balance between play and reading and math, and numbers, academics?

MOTHER 1: For preschool, I think what's most important is learning, not play.

MOTHER 2: More learning.

MOTHER 3: More learning.

MOTHER 1: I think that a little bit more, how do you say that? Knowledge. Wisdom. Like the children in the video, it only showed that they were drawing a drawing, and that was all. I mean, I think that they should teach them more *how* to color, *how* to make crafts.

A group of Mexican parents made similar comments in an interview at a community center in Iowa City:

MOTHER 1: I don't have anything against the preschools. But my Priscilla was in preschool for two years, and she left it having the same knowledge she started with.

INTERVIEWER: Do you mean that they didn't even teach them the colors?

MOTHER 1: No, no, she knew the colors. But, I mean, when you finish preschool, at least you have to be able to know how to write.

MOTHER 2: I don't have anything against her old preschool. But in that place they don't, she didn't even learn the colors. In the school I moved her to, there are fewer children, so they pay more attention to them, and she already knows to write her name. She doesn't know to discern all the colors, but she knows the numbers, she knows the order.

Some immigrant parents in the focus groups expressed very specific ideas about the kinds of academic activities they would have liked to see more of in the preschool curriculum, as evidenced in an extended exchange between Mexican mothers in Riverdale, Iowa:

INTERVIEWER: How did you like the other activities in the video?

MOTHER 1: There was nothing about shapes.

MOTHER 2: Or colors.

MOTHER 3: Or letters.

MOTHER 4: Numbers, there wasn't any of that.

MOTHER 1: That wasn't shown in the video.

INTERVIEWER: Do you all agree about that? What do you think, ma'am?

MOTHER 5: It didn't show any of that.

INTERVIEWER: You mean, for example, you, ma'am, would have liked there to be more, more about shapes.

MOTHER 5: About letters.

INTERVIEWER: And the rest of you?

MOTHER 2: Yes. Give them all of the names and, "Get your name. What's your name?" "The first letter?" The video didn't show even one letter, not one color, or only one, and very little the pronunciation. Just "This color is blue," and that's it.

INTERVIEWER: You all would have preferred that they were teaching directly: "This is this letter," and do it again, many times?

MOTHER 3: I think that would be good.

MOTHER 4: Like: "Now it's Monday, such-and-such a day," or something.

MOTHER 6: To mention the day.

MOTHER 4: The month. Well, they go to school to learn, but they're not teaching them the days of the week. Or the months or what year it is. That's what's important. To me it seems like that is what's missing.

MOTHER 3: Yes, because it just showed playing on the playground and music. Just singing and playing. It's good too, to be singing and to liven up the kids. But it seemed to me there was very little teaching about the letters.

MOTHER 8: I think that while they are awake, teach them as much as you can.

MOTHER 9: They're small for a lot of work. If they would just try to get them to focus a little on the letters and colors.

MOTHER 5: Yeah, it would be good for them to focus on the letters a little bit more. Like, start on the first few letters in their name, because it's difficult for them to remember them all, their whole name, letter by letter.

MOTHER 6: They should learn more, with less play. They should learn more things about the animals, all what a child could learn, all the necessary things.

MOTHER 9: Play helps, but not in excess. It's more about learning.

West African parents at a child care center in Harlem also had specific suggestions for adding rigor to the curriculum:

MOTHER 1: I want to see my daughter learning more. She's sharp, you know, I feel that she is. She can fix things very fast. So I want that to be utilized for her. To be taught the alphabet, math or whatever. She's happy to learn that now, but I don't think that's enough.

FATHER 1: I want to see more structure, lessons, stuff like that and less play. They need to start early, much earlier.

FATHER 2: Like in the French video, the boy Mamadou signed his name on his picture, right? The teacher said, "Mamadou, sign your name," and he wrote his name. My daughter cannot.

MOTHER 2: Yes, they were showing them how to write, I was very impressed with that. I should give them credit, yes. Maybe that's something we can learn from, you know. To have them writing, that's good. It was very much geared towards learning. The French teacher was very strict.

Statements of a desire for more emphasis on academics often were tied, as in these comments, to a preference for more direct and systematic instruction, as well as for more discipline. For example, in a focus group discussion on the Solano video, parents at the Islamic School preschool in Tempe had this to say:

PAKISTANI MOTHER: I don't like the way they did reading time. When they just got books. How is the child supposed to identify the picture with the words? The young boy said to read it to them, and they're pointing things in the book out to her. They understand the comprehension of it, but they don't know the words. I like the computer, with the highlighting of the words as it's going.

TURKISH MOTHER: The children were walking all around. The teacher should have said: "It's time for reading. Sit down and listen to me." To ask them questions, I mean, to be more. . . .

SAUDI MOTHER: Obedient.

In a focus group conducted in English at Solano Preschool with non-Spanish-speaking immigrant parents, there were many expressions of appreciation for the kindness and professionalism of the teachers, but these parents also wanted more academic emphasis, and some questioned the assumptions behind the school's progressive, play-oriented approach:

BOSNIAN MOTHER: It looks like a typical day. But I think a lot of it right now is like socializing and learning about each other and learning different things, how to be in a situation where you have to sit and do different tasks. But I think like fundamentals of writing should probably be introduced at this level. Just the basics, like the As, and the Bs, and not really anything complicated. That's the only thing that's missing.

FILIPINA MOTHER: Just introduce it, like introduce the ABCs. The numbers and stuff.

INTERVIEWER: I think the teacher would say that children learn skills through their play.

BOSNIAN MOTHER: You say when she was playing games, they were learning skills. I don't know how to ask this question, but how do you know they are doing that? Do the kids come home with added skills that you can see? And how do you know they're not just playing games, and that they're learning things too? How do you know that's happening?

This parent raises a deep question that is difficult for teachers and scholars to answer: How do teachers know that their constructivist approaches are working? How can parents know that the play-based curriculum is leading to real learning?

EXPLAINING IMMIGRANT PARENTS' DESIRE FOR MORE ACADEMIC EMPHASIS

The pattern is clear in our data: immigrant parents from a variety of cultural backgrounds, and across all the sites where we conducted focus groups, want less play and more academics in the preschool curriculum. We suggest that a variety of factors contribute to this desire for a greater focus on academics.

Parental Pragmatism and Ecological Decisionmaking

Immigrant parents tend to think pragmatically and strategically about their children's early education. They make calculations (correct or incorrect) about what their children need now, the world they will encounter in both the near and more distant future, and the kind of person they want to see their children become. Both their hopes and their fears figure into these calculations, as does their assessment of the local context in which they live.

We suggest that the preference of many immigrant parents for greater emphasis on academics and on English-language acquisition is based less on a theory of learning than on a pragmatic concern about their child's readiness for kindergarten and the consequences of being behind. Many of the immigrant parents in our focus groups expressed concern about their children's academic readiness for primary school and hoped that the preschool would do all it could to help their children catch up with their non-immigrant peers. Immigrant parents see their children as starting out behind, and they see it as the school's responsibility to help close this gap. As one West African father put it, using a soccer metaphor, "From the day he enters preschool he's already behind 1-nil." Parents see the gap as resulting not just from their children's lack of fluency in the national language when they start preschool but also from their own limited ability to help their children academically in an unfamiliar school system and language. For example, in a focus group in Phoenix, Mexican parents told us that they felt uncomfortable reading books in English to their children and wanted the preschool to compensate for their inability to teach their children to speak, read, and write in a new language. Feeling that they can do a better job with the social and moral education than they can with language and on academic preparation, immigrant parents look to the school to do what they cannot.

Some immigrant parents contrasted the nurturing atmosphere of preschool with the pressure of primary school. As a Bosnian mother in Phoenix said: "The teachers here in the preschool are so nice and caring. But I know it won't be this way next year when my son goes to kindergarten." Concerned about the academic expectations and the strictness to come in primary school, many immigrant parents suggested that toward the end of the preschool year teachers should ramp up the academics and raise their standards for comportment. Many of the immigrant parents in our study emphasized that the stakes would soon be very high for their children, whom they viewed as at risk of ending up failing in the new society in school and in employment if they were not ready to succeed academically when they entered primary school.

Teachers also think strategically and contextually, but as we discuss later, they are more likely to hold beliefs about best practice that transcend contexts and are tied to their professionalism. For immigrant parents, thinking pragmatically means combining their assessment of what they and the school can provide their child, what the primary school will require, and the stakes of falling short.

Social Conservatism

Beliefs about preschool pedagogy are tied to more general beliefs about learning, knowledge, and authority. Immigrants who are members of socially and morally conservative communities tend to hold views on pedagogy and curriculum in which knowledge is transmitted rather than socially constructed and in which adult-child relationships are asymmetrical and thus it is appropriate that children show deference to teachers and other authorities. These values are, of course, not limited to new immigrant communities.

Some preschools that emphasize an academic approach base their curriculum and pedagogy on cultural traditions, beliefs, and practices that predate the development of preschools—for example, the traditional Talmudic, Islamic, and Catholic and Protestant approaches to the religious instruction and rearing of children (on Orthodox Jewish preschools, see Yafeh 2007; on madrasa Koranic schools, see Bartlett 2012). In these traditions, there is an emphasis on respect for the knowledge and role of the teacher, on the mastery of core knowledge, and on moral education. This emphasis is found as well in some secular programs that call for "getting back to basics" and for the orderly teaching and learning of "core knowledge and values" (see, for example, E. D. Hirsch's "core knowledge" preschools).

Disagreements about how and what should be taught in preschool are just one battleground in the much broader culture war that is raging between conservatives and progressives. Proponents of constructivist, play-based approaches accuse the academic, direct-instruction programs of being based on old-fashioned notions and of failing to reflect current knowledge. On the other side, proponents of the academic approach view the constructivist, play-oriented programs as pushing a trendy progressivism, moral and intellectual relativism, and a multiculturalist sentimentality that reflects an abandonment of traditional values and practices.

Studies have shown that preferences for more constructivist versus more didactic approaches to schooling vary considerably by social class and culture. Parents who immigrate from more traditional societies, who are religious, and/or who are from working-class urban or agrarian backgrounds (all of which is true for the majority of the immigrants in our study) tend to hold more conservative views on education than do progressive educators. Studies by Lisa Delpit (1995), Guadalupe Valdes (1996), Annette Lareau (2003), and Joseph Tobin, Yeh Hsueh, and Mayumi Karasawa (2009) show that working-class, African American, and Mexican American parents tend to want more direct instruction than do many white middle-class parents. Some researchers—for example, Lareau (2003) and Rebecca Morton (2011)—emphasize that such illiberal notions of knowledge and authority reduce working-class and immigrant students' educational chances by creating a mismatch between dispositions favored at home and at school. On the other hand, other researchers—for example, Alejandro Portes and Min Zhou (1993), Bruce Fuller (2007), and Vivian Louie (2004)—suggest that that these conservative dispositions can be adaptive. As Fuller (2007, 256) writes:

> What might be seen as illiberal parenting—say, through tight oversight of homework or strict compliance with adult authority—can help to predict school success in many Latino families, according to psychologists Parke and Buriel (1998). The efficacy of particular home practices must be judged in the context of community norms and how such parenting equips a Latino child to perform in what's first seen as a foreign setting.

Conversion Narratives

Memories of their own early schooling experiences contribute to many immigrant parents' conservative views of curriculum. Many parents reported in our focus groups that the schools they attended when they were young were more authoritarian and less constructivist than their child's preschool in the United States. A more academic, more structured approach is therefore what many immigrant parents know and expect when they arrive in their new country.

In preschools that offer parent education, a common narrative we heard in our focus groups was: "When I arrived from Mexico, I didn't appreciate how children learn through play." In many of our focus groups, immigrant parents shared this conversion narrative—that over time they came to see the light and appreciate the virtues of a play-oriented curriculum. For example, at a Head Start center in New York, a mother from Guatemala explained the school's play-oriented curriculum:

> I think that they learn while playing. When they are playing, they aren't just playing. If they are playing with blocks, they are learning what a square is, what a circle is. When they play with modeling clay, they're learning too. When you want them to sit down and be quiet, they don't want to. I think that when they are little they learn best by playing.

In a focus group at Solano, a Mexican mother defended the play-oriented approach of her child's teacher:

When I first came here, I thought there was only playing. But now I learned from Ms. Lolie about how they are learning lots of things when they are playing. It is different than in Mexico; they learn things here, but in a different way. It's better when they are so little that they learn in this way and they are happy when they are learning.

There is a developmental narrative in such accounts of immigrant parents' encounters with the American preschool's play-oriented curriculum: their incorrect notions of how children learn are replaced gradually by more sophisticated understandings. This is a narrative told to us not only by some immigrant parents but also by many teachers, who describe immigrant parents as eventually coming to understand and appreciate the logic of their play-oriented curriculum. Later in this chapter, we present a more complicated perspective on such conversion narratives.

To summarize: the great majority of comments about the curriculum made by immigrant parents in our focus groups express a preference for more academic emphasis in their children's preschools. We suggest that this preference reflects a combination of factors, including immigrant parents' initial unfamiliarity with the play-paradigm of the American preschool; anxiety about their children being at risk of falling behind academically when they start kindergarten; and a socially conservative set of beliefs: children should show respect to teachers, learning requires discipline, and knowledge is transmitted rather than constructed. As we will see, their children's teachers rarely share these beliefs.

TEACHERS

Teachers in many of our focus groups answered our questions about the ideal balance of play and academics by stating that their program "follows DAP" and is "NAEYC-accredited." In using these acronyms, the teachers were signaling their membership in a professional organization and adherence to a set of core professional beliefs. NAEYC is the National Association for the Education of Young Children, an organization that both sets standards for and accredits preschools. Developmentally appropriate practice (DAP) is a compendium of practices that NAEYC recommends for preschool classrooms because these practices are believed to be well matched to children's abilities and interests, consistent with current research and theory in the field, and effective for promoting children's social and emotional as well as academic development (Copple and Bradekamp 2011). The underlying conceptual framework for DAP is constructivism, the belief—as articulated especially by Swiss developmental psychologist

Jean Piaget and Russian psychologist Lev Vygotsky—that young children learn best by engaging with the world around them and by developing and testing their constantly emerging schema and strategies for dealing with, manipulating, and making sense of that world. Practices considered "not DAP" include direct instruction, workbooks, and the "pushing down" of elementary school curriculum and pedagogy to kindergarten and the pushing down, in turn, of kindergarten curriculum and pedagogy to preschool.

In our interviews, teachers frequently complained of feeling pressured to abandon DAP principles from above by No Child Left Behind and school boards, and from below by parents. In many of the focus group discussions, teachers expressed defensiveness and awareness that many parents perceived them as failing to give their children enough academic preparation. In a discussion at an Upper West Side Head Start in New York City, conducted in Spanish, a group of teachers who themselves were immigrants from Mexico, Central America, and the Caribbean explained their position:

TEACHER 1: Parents are always questioning us.

INTERVIEWER: What kind of questions do they have?

TEACHER 1: One is that we don't teach them the ABCs.

TEACHER 2: We teach that, but not formally, not like: "Sit down and this is the letter A and this is the letter B." We do that through playing.

TEACHER 3: Academic playing, yes.

These and other preschool teachers we interviewed made a distinction between formal instruction and learning through play, what Teacher 3 in this example calls "academic playing." A teacher in one of our Phoenix focus groups described this approach as teaching in such a way that "the children [don't] know they are learning." A teacher in Iowa made a distinction between "bad academics" and "good academics," suggesting that preliteracy supported through play is a positive way to bring academic rigor to the preschool curriculum:

I wouldn't say bad academics, but more academics. The good academics, as far as letter awareness and all those things, too, that are important in preliteracy. But it [the play-based literacy program endorsed by her district] also helps support and give administrators the understanding that play is children's work.

This teacher shows awareness that her administrators need help to understand and justify the rationale behind a constructivist pedagogical approach.

Teachers we interviewed in Nashville referred to such an approach as "structured play" and explained that academic skills are better learned via play than direct instruction:

TEACHER 1: I do a lot of academic focus that's just embedded into whatever they're playing. When they have an opportunity to choose different centers, one of the centers I always have is the writing center. So every once in a while I will go and sit in the writing center with them and say, "Okay, I'm going to write a letter to my friend." I just talk about that as I'm doing it. I'm showing them how to do it. And a lot of times they'll imitate it, or do something totally different. All of the things are there for them to do all kinds of writing—papers and all different kinds of writing utensils. I also have letters and numbers all over the room, in all the different centers, so that they are constantly seeing those things in different environments.

TEACHER 2: And it makes it easier for them. They are already familiar with it, and so they come into the centers. Some of the centers are more structured.

At a preschool in Harlem, a group of teachers reported that they usually are able to convince parents of the merits of their play-based approach:

INTERVIEWER: In the video, what did you think about the balance of play and more academic kinds of things?

TEACHER 1: I see that it's definitely through play. I like the way the teachers were fooling around with the children in centers. Like they seem to find time for each child, you know, in different areas. They were enhancing their play by being with them, you know.

INTERVIEWER: That's similar to what you do?

TEACHER 1: Yeah.

INTERVIEWER: Do you ever have parents who say to you that they want more learning of writing and letters and numbers?

TEACHER 2: Some parents want more academics: "I want my child to write more." And you know, there are some foundation things that the child needs to know. So I say, "No, it will happen in time. But there are so many things a child can do to start writing."

INTERVIEWER: Do you often have that kind of discussion with parents? Do they say to you: "We want more writing," and then you have to explain and defend your approach?

TEACHER 1: I just think it's more explaining. Like if they don't know what's going on, then, well, once you make them wise to what's going on, they understand, like, "Oh, okay. Kids are not adults. You've shown us that kids have to go through stages and steps to get to do certain things." So once you explain to them it takes this step for them to do this, they're like, "Oh, all right." Then we say, "And then from that step they can do this." And they're like "Oh, okay." So I think it's more explaining it and helping them understand.

TEACHER 3: We have parent meetings and workshops, where we explain to them that, "when he plays in the block area, it's learning some math concepts." You have to spend much of the year reassuring them that they're going to be able to function when they move out of here, that they're going to do well. In fact, they always come back afterwards very surprised: "Oh, don't you know, my child did so well in school." But you have to convince them, in a way.

INTERVIEWER: And you usually can?

TEACHER 4: Usually you can. You know, you still have that "You guys do a *lot* of playing in that classroom" going on. So we try to inform them as much as possible through the class committee or school workshop, and parents also participate in the education committee, in an advisory capacity.

The verbs "reassure" and "convince" imply that these teachers perceive a resistance by immigrant parents to what they are saying about how children should learn in school, and that to overcome this resistance teachers need to provide parents with ongoing explanations about the wisdom of progressive pedagogical approaches.

Teachers reported to us feeling pushed to do more explicit academic instruction, not only by parents who lacked an understanding of constructivism but also from above, by school boards and legislative mandates to prepare children to succeed on standardized tests and to be ready for the transition to kindergarten. For example, teachers in Nashville explained that even within a child-centered, constructivist curriculum, children still need to learn writing skills and beginning phonics if they are to be ready for success in kindergarten:

TEACHER 1: Well, mostly, we're trying to get ready for kindergarten. Which means, you know, writing skills. We get into some phonics, spelling their names out.

TEACHER 2: Literacy.

TEACHER 1: Literacy.

TEACHER 3: Recognizing letters and numbers and all of it. Math, science, all of it. They're very exposed to all of it. Computers, they're exposed to all of it. We use the kindergarten to see where they need to get to, and then we work towards getting them there.

The Nashville preschool teachers listed a number of academic areas in which they needed to prepare children for school success: literacy, phonics, spelling, letters, numbers, math, science, and computers. It is telling that Teacher 1 said, "*We're* trying to get ready for kindergarten," rather than, "We are trying to get *the children* ready for kindergarten." Her phrase suggests that teachers as well as children and parents are feeling and responding to the pressure for academic readiness.

Many teachers lamented the changes in preschool over the past decade that have resulted from this pressure, as can be heard in these comments by teachers in Riverdale, Iowa:

INTERVIEWER: Have the expectations for you as a teacher changed? What's changed?

TEACHER 1: Accountability. I feel like a lot of what we do in preschool now is what kindergarten used to do.

INTERVIEWER: Why has that happened?

TEACHER 1: It's the test scores.

INTERVIEWER: You have had No Child Left Behind for a while now.

TEACHER 1: It was different. It was very different.

INTERVIEWER: How was it different?

TEACHER 1: I just felt, myself, much more relaxed and now it's just. . . . It's just stressful.

TEACHER 2: I don't feel pressure from the parents. Whatever we do, they're grateful for; however we teach them, they're grateful. But yeah, I feel it from the top down.

TEACHER 3: It's the administration. But then they get it from the state.

TEACHER 1: And pass it on to the teachers.

TEACHER 3: Before, it was, "Yeah, do your own thing."

TEACHER 1: You're allowed to have so many minutes of this, and . . .

TEACHER 4: I've been here a whole whopping three years, and whereas you would think, because it's preschool, early childhood age, their assessments would be more social, emotional, like, "How do they get along with other kids?" And we still have that on the progress report, but it's kind of a lower priority. Now we're assessing on letter recognition and sounds.

TEACHER 1: And literacy and vocabulary.

These Iowa preschool teachers' concerns about preschool becoming the new kindergarten were shared by most of the preschool teachers who participated in our interviews. They felt burdened by the new requirements that they get children ready for a kindergarten curriculum that seems at least a year ahead of what it was a generation ago. They lamented the effect on their pedagogy of school readiness concerns and the ways in which they are being made to test their students. Teachers resent being pressured to prepare children for kindergarten in a way that feels contrary to their own lived, professional knowledge of early childhood education, as was expressed by teachers at a church-based Head Start program in Harlem:

INTERVIEWER: Are you worried about the kids in your classroom when they go to kindergarten or first grade? Do you worry about them being successful or being able to adapt or feeling comfortable there?

TEACHER 1: Yes. You spend a lot of time with the child, and you want the best for any child that you have the privilege of teaching. So you do worry to make sure that when they go to the next grade up that they receive the proper education. And they could function in a large group.

TEACHER 2: It's also so much like a family here, within the school. And every teacher knows every child, almost as if it's their own child. Once they move on out of here, it's so very different. That's what I worry about—that they're going to be taken out of one other culture and put in another place so drastically different. There's nothing we can do that can totally prepare them to leave this type of environment.

Not all of the teachers we interviewed were against a stronger emphasis on academic preparation. The preschool staff members of the Islamic

School in Tempe, Arizona, were the group of preschool teachers in our study who most explicitly questioned the notion that children learn best through play. These teachers explained that their pedagogical approach reflects their Islamic beliefs and the mission of the school to teach about Islam and to introduce the children to reading and writing in Arabic (which is not a language spoken at home by the majority of the children in the school):

TEACHER 1: Even though we're dealing with three-year-olds, we teach Islamic studies and we teach Arabic. I know she [the teacher in the U.S. film] was teaching them bilingual speaking, but we also do Arabic and the Koran. We implement religion; we implement Islamic studies, Arabic.

INTERVIEWER: Starting even with the little ones?

TEACHER 1: Even with the day care children. It's difficult. We do fifteen-minute increments, but they are getting it. Even when we eat, actually I see this as very playful, which is good. But there has to be, I think, a little bit of instruction. I think, even with motor skills, like with writing and tracing. I didn't see any of that in the video. Do they do any of that, or is this just playing the whole day? I think it's important. I'm not saying the whole day, and I'm not saying it's not difficult. I mean, we struggle with it. It's difficult, but it's important.

INTERVIEWER: Do you all agree? Do you think the teachers in the video weren't giving enough instruction or structure to the kids' play?

TEACHER 3: I'm not saying that there needs to be one hour of sitting down writing, but like fifteen minutes.

TEACHER 4: I think instruction is important for my students. I do like at least one hour a day of writing, but it's not the whole hour. It's just like we do fifteen minutes of math, then we paint, then we do twenty minutes of language art. Then they color. And then we do fifteen minutes of Arabic.

These teachers acknowledge the value of play and the need to adjust pedagogy to children's developmental level, but they also see value in direct instruction, even for young children. The hybridity and heterogeneity of their pedagogy can be seen in the way they combine principles of instruction from their Islamic tradition of direct instruction with American play-oriented approaches to early childhood knowledge such as breaking up children's activities into smaller increments and supplying children with a range of daily experiences. These teachers work to balance a traditional, didactic approach to religious instruction, which is what parents expect from an Islamic school, with the professional knowledge valued by the field of early childhood education in the United States.

One of the sites where we conducted focus groups with parents and teachers was a Head Start program on the Upper West Side in New York City. The program originally served a mostly African American community and now serves a mostly Hispanic, new immigrant community from Mexico and Central America. Here, as in many other sites where we conducted research, parents expressed appreciation for the quality of the education and care their children were receiving, but also some frustration with aspects of the curriculum. In a discussion conducted in Spanish, parents expressed support for the program's emphasis on social and emotional development and an understanding of the program's philosophy that children learn best through play. But the parents also told us that they wanted more academics and less play:

INTERVIEWER: Is there anything you would like to see changed here?

MOTHER 1: The most important thing is get them ready for kindergarten.

MOTHER 2: The teachers are very nice, and the playtime is good. But I wish they would work more on their letters.

MOTHER 3: They should know how to write their names, and they should know their numbers.

FATHER 1: Maybe just a little more time on learning their letters and numbers.

MOTHER 1: So they'll be ready for kindergarten.

When we concluded the discussion by asking these parents if there was anything they wanted us to communicate to their children's teachers, one mother said: "Just ask them, 'Would it kill you to teach my child to write her name before she enters kindergarten?'"

We did ask this question in a subsequent meeting with the teachers, whose answer was that to give in to such pressures from parents would mean to go against their professional beliefs and knowledge. In an interview we conducted in Spanish with five of the teachers, most of whom were themselves immigrants from the Dominican Republic, Puerto Rico, and Mexico, they explained their core beliefs:

TEACHER 1: Some parents think that we do not teach the ABCs.

TEACHER 2: We do teach it, but not formally like: "Sit here, this is an A, this is a B," but rather through play.

TEACHER 3: Many parents bring their children to us with the hope that they will learn to read and write here.

TEACHER 1: With the same methods that they learned as children.

TEACHER 2: But we use different methods, because times have changed.

TEACHER 1: For example, back in our country, when they go to school for the first time, most children did not go to Head Start; they just went to kindergarten in a place like Santo Domingo [the Dominican Republic], where the teacher would seat you at a desk, and it's like, "Let's go. Write these letters." They would even hold your hand, you know, to show you how to write the letters. That was really something. The parents who come from another country, like we do, think that when they come here . . .

TEACHER 2: . . . that it should be that way.

TEACHER 1: And they don't understand that the children are learning through play.

These teachers suggest that parents' perspectives reflect the antiquated methods from the old country that they experienced as children, methods they describe as simplistic, mechanistic, and prescriptive.

We returned the next year to share our preliminary findings with the school's director, an African American educator with a master's degree in early childhood education:

INTERVIEWER: In the focus groups here, many of the immigrant parents told us that they want more direct instruction and academic emphasis. Are you aware of this?

DIRECTOR: Yes, of course. We hear this all the time.

INTERVIEWER: What would you say to the idea that you should change your approach to be closer to what the parents want?

DIRECTOR: "We shall not be moved."

The director's invocation here of the key line in the anthem of the American civil rights movement is pointed. This citation of the African American struggle for civil rights (and specifically of Rosa Parks's refusal to move to the back of the bus) suggests that it would, in a metaphorical sense, kill her and her staff of teachers to teach the ABCs, because it would force them to go against their understanding of themselves as early childhood educators and to betray their core professional beliefs.

The contrast between the positions of the parents and the staff was expressed in particularly stark and dramatic terms at this preschool. But we found the same divide at most of the preschools where we conducted focus groups, with teachers declaring the value of a play-based curriculum and warning against the dangers of a "pushed-down" academic approach and immigrant parents (and many non-immigrant parents as well) wishing that their children's preschool would focus more on the direct teaching of letters and numbers.

TEACHERS' FEELINGS OF THREATS TO THEIR PROFESSIONALISM

Teachers who work with immigrant children and their families often find themselves caught between two core professional values: their beliefs in constructivist, progressive pedagogy and their belief in being culturally sensitive and responsive to the families and communities they serve. Most progressive educators are more than willing to bring the culture of the home into the classroom in the form of songs, stories, artwork, holidays, and food. For example, in response to our questions about their willingness to change their practice to accommodate immigrant parents' wishes, teachers with Muslim children in their class often mentioned that they had made dietary allowances for children who did not eat pork.

But when the discussion moved from food and clothing to questions about the curriculum, most teachers became much more resistant to making changes to accommodate parents' wishes.

We suggest that there are several reasons for this resistance. One is that teachers believe that their curricular and pedagogical knowledge is what distinguishes them from parents, and that the power to decide what and how to teach is at the core of their professionalism (Hughes and McNaughton 2000). Most teachers do not conceive of parents' curricular wishes as cultural beliefs that, like beliefs about food, religion, and dress, should be respected or negotiated, but instead as forms of ignorance to be corrected. What happens when early childhood educators see their own beliefs about practice as non-negotiable professional codes that must be followed is that they position parents' wishes as deficits—that is, as misunderstandings in need of correction rather than as ideological differences that deserve discussion and compromise.

We suggest that there are several reasons for teachers' hesitation to engage in discussions and negotiations over the curriculum with immigrant (and other) parents. One is the defensiveness that grows out of teachers' feelings of relative powerlessness—though they are more powerful than immigrant parents, many preschool teachers nevertheless feel vulnerable and disrespected. A related reason is that many teachers may fear losing their hard-won professionalism. To accede to parents' curricular requests might make them appear to other teachers, directors, and evaluators as backsliding and failing to implement the progressive positions in which they were trained.

A related explanation is the zeal of the recently converted. Head Start centers and other public early childhood education programs often recruit classroom aides and teaching assistants from among the parents who have children enrolled in the school. Because most of the preschools that serve children of recent immigrants are such public programs, many of the teachers in our study were themselves immigrants, and many others came from poor and working-class backgrounds. A common narrative told by these teachers is one of having over time come to see the light: though initially they had been critical of the play-oriented approach typical of NAEYC-accredited classrooms, it roused their curiosity, and eventually they became enthusiastic converts. For example, Victoria, who had come to the United States as an immigrant from Mexico ten years earlier, told us:

> When I came here, my daughter was almost four, but in my country she has been in kindergarten since she was two. And already in that program, when she arrived, she already knew the *a, e ,i, o, u,* the vowels, and she knew how to write some words. When we arrived here, I questioned what I saw in the program because I thought, *But they were teaching my daughter more back home than what they are teaching her here.* But at the same time, the fact that I was a volunteer here and I was in the classroom, I started noticing that she was learning, but in another dimension, in another way. At first, I always said, "Ay, ay, ay, she is going to be behind," because I didn't see any workbooks here.

Victoria presents a typical development narrative: as a new immigrant who had just arrived in the United States, she at first was disappointed in what she saw at her daughter's preschool. But gradually, as she spent time in the classroom, first as a volunteer and then as an aide, she came to see the virtues of the play-based approach. In this journey, she had to shed some old beliefs about learning and teaching.

We also suggest that teachers fear that agreeing to enter into dialogue with parents about their practices will open the floodgates and they will have to compromise core beliefs. Teachers and directors hesitate to enter into dialogue with parents about the curriculum because they fear being outnumbered in meetings with parents and fear that immigrant parents will have exotic and unrealistic requests, demands, and expectations.

There is an irony here: progressive teachers hold a constructivist view of working with young children—whom they view as capable of constructing knowledge, as having the right to determine their own interests, and as being more capable and knowledgeable than adults often give them credit for—but they rarely apply this constructivist view to (immigrant) parents. Instead, they often view parents through a deficit perspective, underestimating their knowledge and rejecting their right to have a say about the curriculum.

The Belgian sociologist and early childhood educator Michel Vandenbroeck (2009, 167) eloquently summarizes the dilemma that confronts not only progressive preschool teachers and directors but also the early childhood professoriate and policy community:

> Some ethnic minority parents protest against what they view as a non-academic direction of multicultural curricula and ask for a more "traditional" *magister*, directing the learning and disciplining of the children when necessary. Some parents reject the presence of bilingual assistants or of the home language of the child in the centre. . . . As progressive academics or practitioners, how can we not take into account the perspective of parents who wish to "conform" to standards of academic achievement (or to achieve this cultural capital as Bourdieu could have said), rather than to discuss holistic education? But on the other hand, how can we, if we have consecrated a major part of our lives to child centeredness? As a critical pedagogue I may argue that this parental question of conformity with the dominant norms and values is to be considered as "internalised oppression" (Freire 1970). But then again, wasn't it also Freire who said "Dialogue cannot exist without humility. . . . How can I dialogue if I always project ignorance onto others and never perceive my own?"

Vandenbroeck (2009) here has gone to the heart of the dilemma confronting progressive practitioners and scholars: immigrant parents' preference for more direct academic instruction can be explained as resulting from "internalized oppression" and their lack of familiarity with more constructivist practices, but taking such a stance is self-serving, hierarchical, and counterproductive, as it positions parents as the problem and practitioners and scholars as the solution. Vandenbroeck suggests that this is a dilemma in thinking about effective practices for working not only with parents who are recent immigrants but also with parents who are ethnic minorities, poor, or otherwise perceived to be lacking in social and cultural capital. The ascription of deficits can obscure substantive differences in beliefs about the means and ends of early childhood education and preclude dialogue about the curriculum between parents and practitioners.

REASONS FOR OPTIMISM

Some contemporary early childhood educators argue that the opposition between an emphasis on play and an emphasis on learning is a false distinction and a distraction (Bodrova 2008; Katz 1999) and that the field should advance beyond the paradigm debate and develop understandings of teaching and learning and hybrid forms of early childhood practice that transcend these binary distinctions and combine knowledge and skill mastery with child agency (Lonigan and Phillips 2012; Marcon 2012). In the United States, for example, NAEYC (2009a, 2009b) has recently made subtle but significant changes to its notions of the role of the teacher in a constructivist classroom: it now puts less emphasis on the earlier notion of the teacher primarily creating opportunities for children's self-initiated learning, and more emphasis on the teacher's role in scaffolding children's intellectual, emotional, and social development. These "third way" or "middle path" approaches give some cause for hope that when there is disagreement between parents and teachers, compromise will be possible.

Practitioners' tendency to be pragmatic and parents' tendency to trust and support their children's teachers also provide cause for optimism that differences in views of the curriculum can be resolved through compromise. Even in contexts where the paradigm wars are raging, early childhood practitioners tend to be more pragmatists than ideologues (Tobin et al. 2009). Many employ mixed approaches to the curriculum, pragmatically using approaches based on their sense of what works best for the children in their class. As a result, many preschool classrooms are less ideologically or conceptually pure than might be expected from program descriptions or the guidelines of the professional associations that certify and provide training to the programs.

Many preschool parents—and perhaps especially parents who are recent immigrants—believe that the teacher is the expert on questions of curriculum and pedagogy and that they should not aggressively voice their opinions in this domain. Cultural customs of deference to authority (as we discuss in chapter 4) keep immigrant parents from criticizing their children's school and the approach of its teachers. Teachers may make the error of taking such deference as a sign of agreement.

THE INTERSECTIONALITY OF CULTURE, IMMIGRATION STATUS, AND CLASS

Many of the positions we have presented as characteristic beliefs of immigrant parents are also held by many non-immigrant parents, especially when they are of similar class backgrounds. Studies have shown that many working-class African American (Delpit 1995) and white working-class (Lareau 2003) parents want more direct instruction and teacher authority than do many parents and teachers who have more years of education and higher social class status. Some differences between immigrant parents and teachers that we have ascribed to culture or country of origin could also be ascribed to class.

Although social class has been demonstrated to have a significant impact on educational beliefs and preferences, we would add a proviso: just as we should be careful not to use the category of culture to mask class, we need to avoid using the concepts of culture and class to mask ideological disagreements that transcend these categories. Beliefs about the means and ends of early childhood education cross both cultural and class lines. There are working-class immigrant parents who hold liberal educational views just as there are socially conservative middle-class parents who share with many working-class and immigrant parents a preference for an approach to education that emphasizes respect for teachers and a transmission model of learning. What we have described as the socially conservative pedagogical beliefs and values of many new immigrant parents are also held by many native-born Americans. An irony is that those members of society who tend to be the most anti-immigrant often share with many immigrants socially conservative perspectives on education.

CONCLUSION

The key finding of this chapter is that a gap exists between immigrant parents and their children's teachers on questions of balancing play and academics in the preschool curriculum. Teachers for the most part are aware of this gap, but are usually unable or unwilling to close the gap in any way other than by persuading parents to change their position and join them on their side of the divide. Most teachers are sympathetic to the immigrant children and parents they serve and eager to be culturally sensitive and responsive. But in the end these early childhood educators feel caught between two prime directives: their professional beliefs (for example, in constructivism and other versions of best practice) and their desire to be responsive to immigrant parents and communities. The gaps between what parents are asking for and what best practice dictates are usually not huge, but teachers often perceive them as insurmountable. Most teachers are willing to adapt their practice on issues such as food, clothing, and holiday customs, but around issues of knowledge, pedagogy, and gender and the body, cultural differences become more threatening and firmer lines are drawn.

We have shown in this chapter that progressive teachers have a constructivist view of working with young children, whom they view as capable of constructing knowledge, as having the right to determine their own interests, and as being more capable and knowledgeable than adults generally give them credit for. But these teachers rarely apply this constructivist view to (immigrant) parents and instead often view them through a deficit perspective, disregarding their knowledge about teaching and learning and their children's educational needs as well as their right to have a say in the curriculum.

One implication of this finding is that teachers should discard the deficit perspective and stop seeing parents' requests to modify their curriculum and pedagogy as expressions of ignorance. Our position is that it is both wrongheaded and counterproductive to think of parents' beliefs as forms of ignorance and teachers' beliefs as knowledge. We would suggest that interests, experience, and ideology intersect in the beliefs of both parents and teachers. This is not to say that they are equivalent, or that professional training does not give teachers' beliefs a different standing from those of parents, but rather that this difference in standing does not justify an a priori assumption that parents' preferences for the curriculum are misinformed.

Chapter 4 | Language

OF ALL THE TOPICS DISCUSSED in our interviews with parents and teachers, language was the one that produced the most comments. In focus group after focus group, immigrant parents told us that they were anxious for their children to learn English, but at the same time they worried about their children growing up losing fluency in their home language. We began the project expecting to hear strong support from immigrant parents for home-language preservation and endorsement of a bilingual approach in the preschool classroom. What we found instead was that most parents and some teachers, though worried that children would lose their home language and culture, did not see the school as having a major role to play in preventing such loss.

To understand why the majority of our informants told us they wanted the preschool to concentrate on English as well as why others said they wanted a bilingual approach, we need to pay attention to not only the opportunities for language development in each of the communities where we conducted research but also the constraints on such development. This analysis reveals not a nationwide pattern but instead variation that reflects a combination of factors: the size and cultural heterogeneity of the community and the school where we conducted the interviews, as well as the percentage of new immigrants; the variety of home languages spoken by the children in a class; the community's long experience or only recent experience of receiving immigrants from a particular language and cultural background; the presence or absence of bilingual teachers; and the local and state climate toward immigrants and language policy. In each setting we heard comments about language that may have been not so much expressions of belief about how young children's language development should be supported in an ideal world as practical responses to imperfect situations and urgent concerns.

The context should be kept in mind here: some of the schools where we conducted focus groups had teachers who were bilingual, while others had only English-speaking staff. In some of the schools—like Solano, where we made the video we used as a cue for the focus group discussions—teachers and children switched back and forth throughout the day between English and Spanish. But such mixing of Spanish and English was not the explicit practice of a systematic bilingual program but instead the intuitive practice of the teachers and children. None of the preschools where we conducted focus groups had a bilingual program, and none of the teachers had received systematic training in the strategies of bilingual education.

PRAGMATISM AND IDEOLOGY

Teachers in Nuevo Campo, a town on the border between Arizona and Sonora, Mexico, explained to us that their community was firmly rooted in Mexican culture and Spanish was the language of everyday life. The Nuevo Campo teachers, who were all Hispanic and fully bilingual, told us that their approach to promoting children's language development was to move as quickly as possible from instructing in Spanish to English, so that by the middle of the second of the two preschool years all instruction was in English. When we asked why they felt a need to move by the second year to an English-only approach, the teachers explained (in Spanish):

TEACHER 1: Because they are spoken to only in English when they go to the district (elementary school). So then they have to understand.

TEACHER 2: And we do it as a transition, little by little. Because they are going to enter kindergarten, how it would be for them when they get there if they have to face an unknown language? They won't be able to use their language, their first language.

TEACHER 1: And academically too. If the teacher is teaching something to the child it's going to be difficult, and I mean the child is not going to understand what the teacher is saying.

These preschool teachers moved as quickly as possible from using Spanish to English in their classroom, not because they were philosophically opposed to bilingualism, or because they did not value home-language retention, but because of the realities of preparing children to enter primary school in Arizona, which is mandated to be English only (Wright 2005). These teachers worried that if children did not enter kindergarten fully fluent in English, they would quickly fall behind academically. In addition to the English-only policy of the state of Arizona, Nuevo Campo teachers cited another practical reality that affected their use of language in the classroom: the sociolinguistic context in Nuevo Campo, where most of life was transacted in Spanish. Teachers explained that children spoke Spanish in stores, in church, and with their family and friends and people in Nuevo Campo frequently traveled back and forth between Nuevo Campo in Arizona and Nuevo Campo in Sonora. Given this environment, teachers were confident that children could keep their home language and their "Mexican roots strong."

The teachers in our Nuevo Campo focus group expressed concern about the challenge their students faced in shifting from Spanish to English, and they stressed that the transition needed to be gradual. We heard much the same thing in focus groups we conducted in preschools in and around Phoenix, where the great majority of the students came from Spanish-speaking homes and many staff members were bilingual. This perspective of gradually weaning children from Spanish and introducing English seemed to conflict with the intent of Arizona's English-only policy (Schildkraut 2005; Soltero-González 2008). That policy governs K-12 education and is usually not applied to preschool programs, but it has a deep impact on them, as preschool teachers in Arizona are keenly aware of the consequences for children who enter kindergarten before they are fluent in English (Arzubiaga and Adair 2009; Garcia, Wiese, and Cuéller 2011).

In contrast, teachers in the communities that were new to receiving immigrants or where the percentage of immigrants was relatively low tended to be less sensitive to the need to transition children gradually from their home language to English. This was the case, for example, in a focus group we conducted in a Head Start program in a suburb of Nashville, where teachers criticized the teachers in the Solano video for speaking too much Spanish with the children and debated whether closeness to the border should be a factor in preschools' approaches to language:

TEACHER 1: In Texas and Arizona, it's more of the states that border Mexico.

TEACHER 2: I don't know, though. If you go to my son's class, in kindergarten, and they've got four that are Hispanic. Two don't speak very much English, and two speak limited.

TEACHER 1: But do they speak English at school?

TEACHER 2: Oh yeah.

TEACHER 1: So they have to pick it up somewhere.

TEACHER 1: Well, they go to the ESL class.

Teacher 2 here switched from speaking as a teacher to speaking as a parent of an English-speaking child in a kindergarten class who had classmates who were native Spanish speakers who had learned to speak English, she believed, from attending ESL classes. These teachers suggested that the only compelling reason for a teacher to speak in Spanish would be to communicate with a child who knew no English, but given that the children in the video appear to be bilingual, their teachers' use of Spanish is counterproductive:

TEACHER 2: I know they speak a lot of Spanish, but we're in America. Why don't they speak a lot of American? The kids speak a lot of American. Don't they speak English?

TEACHER 1: They speak English. I see a lot of using Spanish and not English.

INTERVIEWER: So that's different?

TEACHER 3: You would think they would be integrating English in.

INTERVIEWER: So that's something that you didn't like?

TEACHER 2: Well, I mean, I don't agree with it. I think if you live here, you should speak English.

TEACHER 1: It makes it easier.

TEACHER 3: Right, right.

TEACHER 2: I mean, eventually you'll learn it, but she uses a lot of Spanish. I mean, you think she would use more English than Spanish. Cuz they seem to understand her when she was speaking English.

One of the Nashville teachers compared the bilingual teacher in the video speaking Spanish to children with her experience with two Japanese children in her classroom: "We've got a couple of Japanese kids in our class. And the little girl seems to understand a lot more than the little boy does, because sometimes she'll tell him something in Japanese." This teacher made it clear that while she allowed the Japanese child who was more fluent in English to translate for the boy who was less fluent, "here the teachers speak English always."

Like the Nuevo Campo teachers, the teachers in Nashville reasoned that because English is the language of instruction in the public school, the immigrant children in their preschool need to learn English as soon as possible. A difference was that the teachers in Nuevo Campo believed in introducing English little by little in the classroom, while the Nashville teachers made only small concessions, such as allowing one Japanese child to interpret for another. The contexts were also different: the Nuevo Campo teachers had good reason to be confident that their students, who lived in a Spanish-speaking town, would retain their home-language fluency even without the school's help, while immigrant children in Nashville were at greater risk of losing their home-language fluency, a risk that seemed of no concern to the Nashville teachers. The position on language taken by the Nashville teachers reflected an ideological position that English should be the language of the preschool because anyone living in America should be speaking English. These teachers seemed to be unaware that the preponderance of research suggests that an English-only curriculum is an impractical and counterproductive approach to the early childhood education of three- and four-year-old children who arrive at preschool fluent only in their home language (MacSwan and Pray 2005) and that bilingual programs for young children lead to developmental and scholastic advantages (Carlson and Meltzoff 2008).

In the other sites where we conducted focus groups, teachers' ideas about immigrant children's home languages were expressed in a less overtly political form than they were in Nashville. Instead, they embedded their ideas in discussions of pedagogical approaches. One example came in the discussion of a scene in the film when Joshua asks his teacher, Lolie, for help finding the sandals for his doll:

JOSHUA: Hey, where's his chanclas?

LOLIE: Chanclas?

JOSHUA: Yeah.

LOLIE: Here's some chanclas.

JOSHUA (*shaking his head*): No, this chancla.

Lolie here reinforces Joshua's use of a Spanish word. She explains the logic behind this approach:

> If a child comes to us and speaks to us in Spanish, we answer back in Spanish at the beginning. If they speak to us in English, we answer in English. But with time we support them a little more strongly so that they also practice speaking English. But we never force them if they don't want to.

Most of the other bicultural and bilingual teachers we interviewed agreed with this graduated approach. In contrast, many non-immigrant teachers in our focus groups said that when immigrant children used their home language in the classroom, they responded by supplying the English word. For example, a teacher in Iowa commented critically on Lolie's approach in the chanclas interaction:

> Until they get used to the English, we do a lot of modeling for the kids that don't speak English. Instead of like saying in Spanish, "I'm done!" we'll say, "Okay, you know, say, 'May I be excused.'" We do a lot of that modeling and word for word so they can start picking up the language.

The Anglo teachers in Nashville and Riverdale as well as many of the U.S.-born teachers we interviewed in Phoenix and New York indicated that they usually responded to a child's use of a word from their home language by encouraging them to say it English. This finding suggests a stark difference between non-immigrant and immigrant teachers in their approaches to working with English-language learners (Adair 2011).

BILINGUALISM AND HOME-LANGUAGE RETENTION

The majority of immigrant parents we interviewed across the sites expressed the desire that their children be fully bilingual. For example, in a focus group in Nashville, a Mexican mother commented: "El que habla dos idiomas es, vale por dos" ("He who speaks two languages is worth two [people]"). The similar phrase "El que habla dos lenguas vale por dos" is often used in Spanish-language television and radio advertisements in the United States for language learning products that target immigrants. The message in these ads that bilingualism is a pathway to financial success is echoed in immigrant parents' desire that their children be bilingual.

Immigrant parents gave many reasons for the importance of their child not only learning English but also maintaining their home-language fluency: communication with relatives would be facilitated; their children would be better able to stay connected with their culture; they need their children's help as translators; and bilingualism is likely to be an asset for their children in finding employment when they grow up. Sadness about their children's real or anticipated first-language loss was connected to each of these parental concerns, and more generally to a sense that to lose one's home language is to lose one's culture and one's roots. As a Mexican immigrant father said in a discussion in Phoenix: "It's important that they maintain their roots, maintain the language."

In some of the focus group discussions, immigrant parents worried about home-language loss for their children once they entered school and used the verb "conservar" (preserve) to refer to their children's use of the home language, suggesting that the home language was something valuable, fragile, and at risk of disappearing. As a Mexican mother in Riverdale lamented: "It's sad when it's just one language, because I have my son, he attends a special class. He's a special child [child with a disability], and my child can't even say one single letter he knows in Spanish, not even one."

Such expressions of sadness and worry about home-language loss were voiced most often and most fervently in the newer immigrant communities, such as Riverdale, and in settings where immigrants felt outnumbered and misunderstood, such as the Harlem preschool attended by the children of West African immigrants.

The literature on first-language maintenance among immigrant children suggests that many either will fail to develop fluency in the home language or will become fluent in the home language and then gradually lose it as they grow up and become dominant speakers of the host-country language (Fillmore 1991; Garcia 2005; Kouritzin 1999; Pease-Alvarez 2002; Qin 2006; Soto 2007). Apparently unaware of this research, many of the immigrant parents we interviewed expressed confidence that their children would retain their home language. Even many of the immigrant parents who worried about language loss expressed confidence that *their* children would be fluent in their home language because *they* emphasized it in the home. Parents highly value their children's ability to speak the home language; they just can't imagine that their child will ever stop doing so. This confidence is understandable considering the child's age and life experience. For example, immigrant parents who have just moved to New York City from the Dominican Republic, who have a four-year-old child who until recently spoke only Spanish, who speak very little English themselves, and who see their child only in the context of home, where she is a fluent Spanish speaker, have difficulty imagining that their child will ever stop speaking Spanish fluently. Most of the immigrant parents in our focus groups spoke of first-language learning and retention as "automatic," a belief akin to the notion put forward by many parents that "children are little sponges" who easily absorb whatever they are exposed to.

When immigrant parents in focus groups told us that they worry about their children losing their first language, our knowledge of the scholarship on first-language loss in second-generation immigrants led us to ask them if they were not at least a little worried about their children's home-language retention. When pressed in this way, some parents responded with examples of older children in their neighborhood or children of relatives they knew who refused to speak in their home language with their parents and grandparents. But they usually quickly added that they thought it unlikely that this could happen with their child.

MOTHER 1: There is a boy on my street who won't speak Spanish to his mother. She talks to him in Spanish, and he answers in English.

INTERVIEWER: So are you afraid that your children will lose their language?

MOTHER 1: No. I don't think that they are going to lose it, because that's what I speak.

When we pushed immigrant parents in our focus groups by asking the follow-up question, "You have *no* concern about them losing their language?" some of them responded, not with expressions of concern about their own children, but with stories about language loss in children in *other* immigrant families:

MOTHER 3: I have two nephews who have been living here since they were little, and now they don't want to speak in Spanish at their house. When they talk and watch a movie and do homework, they are speaking in English, and when they talk to their mother, they do it in English, despite the fact the parents are Latino and speak Spanish.

INTERVIEWER: Are you afraid that they maybe are going to lose their language? That they are going to lose their Spanish?

MOTHER 2: They won't lose it if we speak it at home and demand they speak in Spanish.

A typical pattern in the focus group discussions was that immigrant parents first resisted the idea that their children would lose their first language. Then, when pushed, they shared stories of children in other families who indeed had lost their first language. Finally, they concluded that this fate would not happen to their child. The frequency and fervor of such expressions of confidence varied across locales. From those in settings with small immigrant communities or in areas where few people spoke their home language, we heard fewer expressions of confidence and more of concern. In settings that were homogeneous in language and culture of origin, we heard expressions of greater confidence. For example, in Queen Creek, a small town outside of Phoenix that is home to a community of migrant workers from several neighboring Mixtec-speaking villages in Oaxaca, parents told us that their children spoke Mixtec at home and learned Spanish as well as English at school. These parents' confidence was high that their children would learn both Spanish and English at school while maintaining their indigenous language. This confidence in their children's home-language retention was based in part on the cohesiveness and homogeneity of their Mixtec community in Queen Creek and in part on the fact that many of the families spent some months each year back home in Mexico. Although parents in other sites mentioned making occasional trips back home with their children, this was the only site where such visits were described as more routine. Our sense is that families without legal status are hesitant to risk making such journeys, while for documented immigrants from Africa, Asia, and the Middle East the cost of such trips home is too high to do regularly.

Nuevo Campo, Arizona, is a special case: this is a community of Spanish speakers who enjoy daily interaction with their sister city of Nuevo Campo Rio Colorado, just across the river in Mexico. For this reason, parents and teachers in Nuevo Campo expressed confidence that their children would grow up fluent in Spanish. Their chief worry about language was that their children would fall behind children in communities with more Anglos in becoming fluent in English.

Immigrant parents in Iowa were less confident about home-language preservation. Although they, like most of the immigrant parents in our study, told us that they took responsibility for teaching their children their home language, they worried about their children growing up feeling estranged from Mexican culture and not being able to communicate with relatives back home. The possibility of their children losing the native language felt worrisome and even shameful to these parents. As a Mexican mother in Riverdale said: "They don't know Spanish, and this isn't good. And who is embarrassed? The one that didn't teach them Spanish." A Mexican parent living in a neighborhood of Phoenix with few Spanish speakers commented: "My children don't speak Spanish. It's bad because people judge me because of this."

Dominican and Ivorian immigrant parents we interviewed in New York City lamented their children's drifting away from the home language, a drift they associated with a loss of culture and tradition. Arabic-speaking families at the Islamic preschool in Tempe expressed similar worries about their children losing their first language and being exposed to bad morals in public schools. They told us that they enrolled their children in the preschool of the Islamic School not so much because they were concerned about home-language loss, but so that their children could learn "the religious home language of Arabic" and strengthen their Islamic identity.

CRITIQUES OF BILINGUAL EDUCATION

Although they valued their children's opportunity to grow up bilingual, many immigrant parents in our focus groups criticized the bilingual teaching shown in the Solano video and expressed a preference for an English-only approach in their child's preschool. This response surprised us, as it seemed inconsistent with immigrant parents' expressed desire for their children to retain the home language and stay connected to the home culture, as well as with the advantage they saw in children being bilingual.

In some focus groups, parents and teachers brought up logistical impediments that would make a bilingual program impractical in their setting. Parents as well as teachers said that while a bilingual approach such as the one shown in the video might be desirable, it would be impractical in their locale owing to the unavailability of trained bilingual teachers. Immigrant parents in a New York preschool serving immigrants from several different cultural and language backgrounds said that a bilingual approach such as the one shown on the Phoenix video would not be practicable in their own setting, where the approach would have to be multilingual rather than bilingual. One such setting was the Tempe Islamic preschool, where teachers pointed out that a bilingual approach would be impractical given the number of home languages spoken by their students:

TEACHER 1: There are more than Spanish and English speakers in this country. There are more languages, so if we want to teach each single person his own language, we are going to be teaching nothing but languages. We have about fifteen languages in this school. Imagine if we had to teach every single student his own language. We would need a teacher for every one.

TEACHER 2: I don't know how to solve this. If you have the majority speaking in Spanish, and in the classroom you have other languages also spoken by children, and then you go between only two languages, I don't know what this is going to do to the other kids who don't speak the second language.

Acknowledging the impracticability of a multilingual approach, some immigrant parents as well as teachers argued for the value of children being taught at least to say "Hello" in all of the home languages of the classroom. For example, a Turkish mother at the Islamic School in Tempe reasoned that the children in the video who come from homes where a language other than English or Spanish is spoken would have felt less left out if they heard some familiar words in the classroom:

I wish they had some more of the languages, like Vietnamese or Chinese. I wish they had someone, so at least they would learn how to say "Good morning" in Vietnamese, or only say "Hi" in Chinese. This way you would not be left out. And that's what we do when they come in here, "Salaam alaikum," you know, that's the greeting in Arabic. If they did that, students would start to know all the people and the world, not just Spanish and Americans.

Other reasons given by immigrant parents for their ambivalence about bilingual programs and for prioritizing second-language learning over first-language retention included concern about interlanguage confusion and confidence in their children's first-language retention. Their concerns are not supported by the research literature, which suggests that interlanguage confusion is rare, that bilingual programs aid academic performance, and that many children of immigrants lose or never develop full fluency in their home language (Lindholm-Leary and Borsato 2006; MacSwan and Pray 2005; Tse 2001; Fillmore 1991).

One take on the parents' preference for a monolingual program is that they may have been misinformed and were suffering from a form of false consciousness characteristic of what Ingrid Gogolin (2002) calls "the monolingual habitus." This perspective, which can dominate the thinking about language learning of non-immigrants and immigrants alike, assumes that it is only "natural" that everyone who lives in a country should speak a single language. Will Kymlicka (2001, 24) argues that monolingual habitus encourages "citizens to view their life chances as tied up with participation in common societal institutions that operate in the English language."

It is undoubtedly true that most immigrant parents (like most people who are not linguists, bilingual education specialists, or sociologists of immigration) are largely unaware of scientific research findings on language acquisition, language retention, and bilingual education. But we suggest that it is wrongheaded and counterproductive to conceive of immigrant parents' preferences for a monolingual program as a deficit and as an expression of ignorance. It is possible that even if immigrants were given a seminar on this professional literature, they would still choose monolingual programs for their children based on what we are calling pragmatic concerns, a strategic calculation of risks, and a hierarchy of needs.

ECOLOGICAL PRAGMATISM

When pushed to explain why they were not more eager for a bilingual program for their child and why they were not more concerned about home-language loss, some immigrant parents responded with pragmatic reasoning. For example, some parents said that in an ideal world, where their child would live in a bilingual society and attend a bilingual primary school, they would prefer a bilingual preschool. But given the reality that in a few months their child would be moving on to a primary school that was not bilingual and where the costs of being less than fluent in the national language would be high, a bilingual program felt like a luxury they could not afford. The loss of the home language felt like a less pressing risk than the immediate risk of failing to attain second-language fluency in the short time left before primary school. As a Mexican mother said in a focus group in Riverdale, Iowa: "My child already came to preschool behind because he doesn't speak English—if he doesn't learn to speak as well as the other children, he will be in trouble next year when he begins primary school."

This and similar comments suggest not that immigrant parents do not value bilingualism or do not see the virtues of a bilingual preschool program in an ideal world, but that such concerns are trumped by their more urgent pragmatic concern that their child become fluent in English in preschool so as to avoid stigmatization the following year in an English-only kindergarten classroom (Souto-Manning 2007).

Parents' preference for an emphasis on English in their children's preschools therefore can be seen as an expression of a Maslowian hierarchy of needs—they want their children to retain the home language, but they perceive English fluency as the more pressing need if their children are to be kept out of special education and off of low tracks in kindergarten. As Lucinda Pease-Alvarez (2002, 24) concludes about the Mexican immigrant parents she interviewed in a community in a town in northern California:

> They did not appear to hold as high an expectation regarding children's Spanish-language proficiency as they did for their English-language proficiency. When citing reasons for this discrepancy in their linguistic aspirations, parents referred to either the need for their children to learn English well so that they could participate in public life and obtain good jobs or the inadequate Spanish-language learning milieu available to children in their homes and schools.

While we think it is wrong to dismiss parents' preference for monolingual programs as a form of ignorance, we also believe that many immigrant parents underestimate the chance that in a monolingual program their child will lose home-language fluency. To say that parents are pragmatic is not the same as saying that their calculations of risks and benefits are always accurate.

ROLE AND TASK DIFFERENTIATION

Parents in many focus groups said that it was their responsibility to promote their children's first-language retention and the school's responsibility to teach their children English. As a Mexican father said in a discussion in Phoenix: "It is the school's job to teach my child English; teaching him Spanish is my job." A Mexican mother in Mesa voiced the same sentiment:

> I think that the parents are the ones in charge of the language. But while the children are in the school, the teacher is the one in charge of the language, because the child is there. He's learning there, from the teacher and the language he is being surrounded by. Outside of the school it's the parents' charge. The language of each family.

Mexican mothers in Iowa concurred:

INTERVIEWER: Are you afraid your children will lose their Spanish?

MOTHER 1: That depends on us, not the teachers. I have to pay attention so my son learns Spanish. I'm not leaving the teachers to do it for me. They don't have the responsibility for that. If I want my son to learn it, that's my duty, not the teacher's.

MOTHER 2: It depends on you. You need to educate them about the culture, to talk about the country, the place we come from.

This logic leads to a "separate spheres" view of early childhood language development, with school the place for English and home the place for the mother tongue.

This approach was supported by teachers in some of the focus groups, as in a discussion in a Phoenix preschool:

TEACHER 1: I wish I knew more Spanish but I don't, only some words. I understand more than I can say. So I mostly talk to the children in English, even when they talk to me in Spanish.

TEACHER 2: That's okay. They need that from us. They are in school with us for such a small amount of time, just a couple of hours a day, like ten hours out of their whole week. The rest of the time they are speaking Spanish. So when they are with us, that's when they need to be hearing and using their English.

In a discussion in Mesa, Arizona, Mexican mothers made similar points:

MOTHER 1: A teacher told me: "You should force them at home to speak Spanish with you, because the school is only in English, and they have to learn your language. It means: "Force them to speak Spanish so they don't lose it."

MOTHER 2: That means that it's *your* responsibility.

MOTHER 1: Yeah.

MOTHER 3: Is this the parents' responsibility?

MOTHER 2: Yes, because many of them do lose it. Many immigrants' children really, they lose the language. They only speak English, and when they go there [to Mexico] to visit, they don't know.

THE DESIRE FOR A BILINGUAL STAFF MEMBER

Many immigrant parents told us that they highly value teachers who speak their language. At first we took such statements as expressions of support for a bilingual program. Eventually we came to see that parents had other reasons for desiring a bilingual staff. Many of the immigrant parents who told us that they favored an emphasis on English in the preschool want a teacher who speaks their language to facilitate their child's adjustment to preschool. As a Mexican mother in Iowa stated: "It would be great to have a staff member who would understand him when he first starts school when he says he has to go to the bathroom." A mother in Phoenix said: "I feel scared if I go someplace where everyone, no one speaks my language. Think about how it must feel to small children if we leave them at a school where no one understands what they say."

Immigrant parents also see bilingual staff members as advocates for their children. In preschools where there were few or no staff members who were from their culture and who spoke their language, parents expressed concern that there was no one at school to look out for their children. For example, in her reflections on a scene in the video in which the teacher intervenes in a dispute between two girls over a dress in the dramatic play area, a Mexican mother in Mesa expressed concern for how her daughter might be treated as a minority at the school:

I have a daughter. The problem is that in her previous school, there wasn't a Spanish-speaking person. At the beginning, she cried a lot because all her classmates spoke English very well and she didn't. Sometimes that's why they take advantage of them, because they don't know how to defend themselves. They don't know how to answer. That's what happened with the girl with the dress, right? They were fighting for the dress. Maybe the teacher should have taken the dress away from them and not give it back to either of them, right? But in the end, one of them got it. That is, when the two girls were fighting for the dress. It's the same when a child who just enters the school, and who speaks only Spanish, the other children take advantage of them, and they don't know how to defend themselves. They don't even know how to tell the teacher that a child hit him, that a child took something from him, because he doesn't, the teacher doesn't understand him, because she doesn't speak the language; she doesn't speak Spanish. I think that's the problem for us here in the preschools.

This mother argues that because the teacher in the video does not know Spanish, the Spanish-speaking child who is wronged in the dispute is not treated fairly. She blamed this injustice on language, explaining: "The teacher doesn't understand them because she doesn't speak the language." This mother was so concerned with what she saw as an injustice suffered by a Spanish-speaking child that she forgot for the moment that the teacher in the video is bilingual in Spanish and English. This slip suggests that this mother was reflecting simultaneously on the scene in the video and on her own daughter's difficulty in a preschool where no one spoke Spanish. In our focus groups, immigrant parents whose children attended schools where there were no immigrant teachers shared this concern that their children's monolingual teachers would not understand what was happening in interactions among Spanish-speaking children and that teachers without immigrant experience would lack sensitivity to how immigrant children struggle to communicate in a second language. Immigrant parents in these settings believed that a bilingual staff is necessary not so much for home-language preservation as for support and advocacy for their children.

The other reason immigrant parents gave for wanting a teacher who spoke their language was to ensure that they, the parents, could be understood, respected, and not underestimated. For example, Mexican parents at Solano Preschool expressed appreciation for the support they received from the two Spanish-speaking teachers. One mother said:

The teachers treat us well and we feel good here. I feel good here because I can talk and ask freely about what I need to do, about the papers they give us, which are written in both Spanish and English. And when I have a concern, I trust them, I feel good with them. They haven't ever given me a reason to feel bad here.

In our focus groups, immigrant parents told us about misunderstanding things teachers said to them in English, being confused by comments made at meetings by English-speaking parents, and being offended when their children were asked by teachers to serve as translators at parent-teacher conferences. ("How can we speak as adult to adult when our words are translated by a small child?")

Having a teacher from their culture who speaks their language is seen as valuable by parents even when the curricular approach is not bilingual, because it allows them to be more fully engaged in their children's education. Research suggests that as well as making parents feel more comfortable, a bilingual teacher contributes to better educational outcomes for immigrant children. For example, a study by Claude Goldenberg and Ronald Gallimore (1995) shows that Mexican immigrant children do better academically when the classroom teacher is Latina. The regression analysis they conducted suggests that this effect is mostly due to the ease of communication and trust between teachers and parents and to parents' confidence that the teachers understand and respect parental beliefs.

A LACK OF TRAINING IN BILINGUAL EDUCATION

Like some parents, some teachers expressed concern that a bilingual or multilingual environment in their classroom would lead to language confusion. Comments by teachers suggest that most of them worried much more about second-language acquisition than first-language loss. Like the parents, most teachers believed that immigrant children who did not become fluent in English before they entered primary school were at grave risk of educational failure. A consistent finding across settings and across both the parent and teacher discussions is that the ability of immigrant children and parents to speak English was seen as the key marker of successful integration into American society, and an inability (or unwillingness) to do so was taken as the paradigmatic sign of an immigrant's failure (Gogolin 2002).

Although everyone we interviewed saw the teaching of English as a key task of preschools that served immigrant children, there was little agreement or clarity on how this task should be accomplished. At the time of our interviews, none of the preschool sites had an official bilingual program. No teacher reported having received explicit training or guidance in how best to support young children's acquisition of English as a second language. Teachers who were bilingual said that though they sometimes spoke to immigrant children in their home language, they had no systematic way of supporting the children's bilingualism, beyond the strategy used by the teachers in Nuevo Campo—and elsewhere—of gradually transitioning from Spanish to English. In Phoenix, Nuevo Campo, and New York, Spanish-speaking teachers reported using a mix of English and Spanish. French-speaking teachers in New York used their French to communicate with West African immigrant families and children. In the Islamic preschool in Phoenix, where teachers and students spoke a variety of languages at home, including Serbian, Indonesian, Urdu, Turkish, and various dialects of Arabic, Koranic Arabic was introduced as a third language and used for part of the day in the classroom. Each of these sites with bilingual staff maintained a belief in the utility and value of teachers at times communicating with children in their home language, but the much greater emphasis was placed on English-language acquisition. Paradoxically, there was little or no attention paid to strategies for promoting this process.

In addition to expressions of empathetic concern for non-English-speaking children, some teachers expressed frustration that their jobs were made more difficult by having to deal with children who came to them from homes where English was not spoken. Other teachers were undaunted by this challenge, saying that in their experience young immigrant children typically made rapid strides within a few months of entering their program toward becoming fluent in the new language.

What was common to nearly all of the teachers in this study is that they were largely unaware of the research literature on language learning and they lacked adequate preparation for the task of working with second-language learners. Whether or not they themselves spoke more than one language, and whether or not they worked in a monolingual or bilingual classroom, most teachers' decisionmaking about how to work with second-language learners was not informed by research or training. In the words of a Mexican American teacher working in a bilingual classroom in Phoenix, in response to being asked where she learned her techniques of bilingual education: "I didn't really learn it anyplace, if you mean like in the university or somewhere. No one taught me how do to this. I just kind of make it up as I go. I try things, and see if they work, and if they don't, I try something else."

For preschool teachers, lack of adequate preparation in bilingual education is the norm rather than the exception (Beller 2008). Diane Early and Pamela Winton found in their 2001 study that only 10.6 percent of four-year degree programs in early childhood education required a course in working with bilingual children or children with limited English proficiency. Chi-Ing Lim and her colleagues (2009) report in their more recent paper that the situation has improved a bit, with 14 percent of programs now requiring at least one undergraduate course and the majority of other programs including some coverage of bilingualism and English-language learning in other courses. The content of such courses and units varies greatly: Arizona, for example, requires teachers in public programs to have had a course, not in bilingual education, but in "structured English immersion" for English-language learners.

A BATTLE OVER BILINGUALISM IN RIVERDALE, IOWA

In Riverdale, several scenes in the Solano Preschool video that show children and teachers speaking Spanish prompted discussion among the teachers as well as the immigrant parents. In one scene, a teacher is talking in English to a small group of native Spanish-speaking children. They are working on English vocabulary and going back and forth between the English word and the Spanish equivalent. At one point a child uses the word "hongo," and the teacher replies "Sabes que? No podia recordar en mi mente la palabra para 'mushroom'" ("You know what? I couldn't remember in my mind the word for 'mushroom'"). During attendance-taking at circle time, an English-speaking girl is called on, and she tries to answer in Spanish. Encouraged by her teacher, who says, "You almost got it—try again!" the girl says, "Aqui estoy." These scenes prompted discussion among the Riverdale parents and teachers about the fate of the bilingual program in their preschool, which had ended the previous year. Several of the Mexican parents ruefully stated that it was their fault that the bilingual program ended because they had not attended the school district meeting to advocate for it as they should have. As one mother said:

> What happens is that when there is a meeting like this, people don't show up. Because when we were asking to not take away the bilingual program, how many came? Ten people, and there's a lot more of us, more than three hundred people, and nobody came, and that's why they got rid of it. We don't support each other amongst ourselves. They got rid of the bilingual program because people didn't come.

Other parents pointed out that the meat-processing factory where most of them worked would not have let them off to attend an afternoon meeting, but this did not erase the sense of collective guilt and responsibility for losing the bilingual program for preschoolers.

The Riverdale teachers also told us about the demise of the bilingual program. When we asked what had precipitated the closing, one teacher commented sarcastically: "I think it's called No Child Left Behind and test scores." Other teachers agreed, explaining, "It's the data, the accountability issue, really." The immigrant parents took responsibility for the loss of the program. The teachers, in contrast, took no responsibility for the closing and seemed to view the loss of the program as inevitable in the era of No Child Left Behind. They gave no indication that they were aware of the shame and guilt felt by the Mexican parents over the program's demise.

CONCLUSION

On questions of language, as with academic preparation, immigrant parents make pragmatic decisions. We have seen in this chapter that their preferences for how English and home languages should be handled in preschool are based not so much on ideological positions as on calculations of what is feasible, practical, and necessary. These calculations reflect their assessment of the linguistic opportunities and demands of their local communities and schools.

Parents and teachers in Nuevo Campo, on the Arizona border with Mexico, said that their children needed to learn and practice English at school because they lacked sufficient access to English in their daily lives within the community. Some Mexican parents living in heavily Spanish-speaking communities in Phoenix also stressed the urgency of children's English-language acquisition. Although they felt inadequate to the task of teaching their children English, both of these groups of parents were confident that they could pass Spanish on to their children. Parents in smaller immigrant communities in Phoenix, such as the Islamic School preschool in Tempe, expressed greater concern about first-language loss than about second-language acquisition and took steps to get additional support for their children to maintain their home language. Parents from newer immigrant groups, such as those from West and North Africa whom we interviewed in Iowa, Phoenix, and New York, worried about their children growing up to reject their traditions and home language. Mexican parents in Riverdale, Iowa, worried both that their children were at risk of falling behind academically if they didn't become fluent in English in preschool and that their children were at some risk of losing fluency in their first language.

In every locale, parents wanted their children both to maintain their home language and to learn English, but their calculations on which of these tasks was more difficult and how each task should be accomplished varied from one context to another. Phoenix parents had to contend with the effects on their children of English-only laws. New York parents from newer immigrant groups struggled to find resources in their schools and communities to support their home language and culture. Mexican parents in Iowa were confronted with the possibility that their children would lose their Spanish fluency because they lived in a small town whose school had only English-speaking teachers and no bilingual program and where the nearest large Mexican community (in Chicago) was more than a four-hour drive away.

Immigrant parents in each of the cities and schools where we conducted interviews calculated the opportunities and constraints of their political and social environments, and these calculations guided their judgments about the role of their child's school in English acquisition and home-language maintenance. Teachers' views on language varied according to their own experiences with immigration and the contexts in which they worked. And finally, across locations, teachers reported having little or no preparation for the task of working with English-language learners.

Chapter 5 | Identity

IMMIGRANT PARENTS BROUGHT TO DISCUSSIONS of identity a sense of idealism mixed with a pragmatism that reflected their assessment of the opportunities and constraints of the communities in which they had settled. Across our research sites, immigrant parents told us they want their children to become Americans, but also to maintain ties to their cultural roots. For example, Mr. Mohamed, an Egyptian father in Tempe, Arizona, suggested that his children needed to balance becoming active citizens in their adopted land with fidelity to their home culture's values:

> This is my personal opinion. What I don't want in my children, is, ah, I wanted them to preserve the values. But I wanted them, at the same time, to become a participant citizen in this country. So I wanted them to learn the culture that they live in, and if it's not contradicting to my values, I'm okay with even having them in that pot.

Mr. Mohamed's comment that he accepted the necessity of his children being in "that pot" can be read either as a reference to the metaphor of America as a cultural melting pot or as a more general acknowledgment that people of different cultural backgrounds who live alongside each other inevitably intermingle, like ingredients in a stew. His attitude toward such mingling seems more resigned than enthusiastic, as indicated by the word "even" in the phrase "I'm okay with *even* having them in that pot." In light of the anti-immigrant political climate in Arizona and the larger anti-Muslim climate of the nation, Mr. Mohamed acknowledged that his children need to be "participant citizens" in order to assimilate into American society. This pragmatic concern was outweighed, however, by his desire that his children preserve the values he considers most important. Mr. Mohamed's use of the past tense in the phrases "I *wanted* them to preserve the values" and "I *wanted* them to become a participant citizen in this country" convey a hint of ruefulness and suggest a fear of loss of control over his children's identity, a fear voiced by many immigrant parents in our focus groups.

Although many of the perspectives on identity expressed by immigrant parents in our focus groups were consistent from location to location, we also found systematic variation, which we attribute both to differences in the immigrants' cultural, class, and religious backgrounds and to characteristics of their receiving communities. Immigrant parents in our focus groups brought to discussions of religious, civic, and cultural identity the same kind of ecological pragmatism they brought to questions of school readiness and bilingualism, as detailed in the previous chapters.

In this chapter, we show how immigrants' perspectives on identity, culture, and experiences of prejudice take different forms in New York City, where immigrants live in the midst of heterogeneous communities accustomed to immigration, but with high rates of poverty and stressors that include the challenge of finding affordable housing; in a small town in Iowa, where a homogeneous Mexican immigrant community is endeavoring to settle into a rural Anglo society unaccustomed to receiving immigrants; in Tennessee, where long-established African American and European American communities are confronting a sudden increase in their immigrant population; in Phoenix, where the great majority of new immigrants are Hispanic, where there is a sizable native-born Hispanic population, but where anti-immigrant rhetoric and harsh police practices make life precarious; and in Nuevo Campo, a small town on the Mexico-Arizona border where almost everyone speaks Spanish and identifies as Mexican, and where American culture sometimes feels far away.

RESISTING NEGATIVE FEATURES OF AMERICAN CULTURE

At the Islamic School in Tempe, Mrs. Kahn, a Pakistani mother of a four-year-old boy, expressed the belief that preserving home cultural values would allow her child to succeed in and contribute to American society:

> I think it's important that everyone is still intact with their own individuality, and still able to bring something to the community. I admire and I love and I stand in awe of people who are truly, ah, like the Japanese, the Chinese, the Jews, the Muslims, whoever you can think of, who still have that type of family intact. And still be able to come into the community, produce and go back home, and still have their own-ness. There are some cultures, though I shouldn't say cultures, I should say some individuals, and then they end up

coming here and it gets all mixed up because everything is so free and everything is so liberal and I think it's just all hogwash. But I think if we stuck to home, what is true, and still be able to put forth good in our community, it would still outshine the rest, I think.

This immigrant parent argues that if parents are not vigilant, children can become contaminated by liberal "hogwash." To avoid this fate, parents must keep family values intact and hold on to their "own-ness." The challenge is to find the right balance between individuality, family, and community. She praises earlier immigrant groups, including Jews and Chinese, who even after many generations in the United States have managed to hold on to their identity and cultural traditions. Her perspective fits with what Alejandro Portes and his colleagues call "selective acculturation," which they define as a stance toward immigration in which parents attempt to keep their children's values aligned with those of their country of origin (Portes and Zhou 1993; Portes, Fernandez-Kelly, and Haller 2005). Like Mr. Mohamed, Mrs. Kahn wants her children, as they interact with American society, to maintain their Pakistani cultural values, which she believes will buffer them from what she sees as the lax moral values of the United States.

Immigrant parents living in impoverished urban areas expressed concern about their perceptions of the danger of their children being drawn into the values of American adversarial subcultures. For example, in our focus groups in Harlem, immigrant parents from West Africa and the Caribbean worried about their children's attraction to the African American oppositional youth culture of their neighborhood. As a father from West Africa commented: "Bad stuff all around here, drugs, alcohol drinking, kids not go to school. Some of my friends, their kids already older, they get into all kind of stuff."

This and other comments made in our focus groups by African and West Indian parents in Harlem are consistent with what Portes and his colleagues term "segmented assimilation," which suggests that children of new immigrants who attend school alongside American-born children who take an adversarial stance toward the larger culture and schooling are at risk of downward assimilation. Comments made by our West Indian informants in Harlem echoed those of the immigrant parents whom Mary Waters (1999) interviewed in her study of West Indians in New York City. They had arrived in the United States with optimistic attitudes about race and upward mobility through education, but then grew increasingly pessimistic and bitter as they discovered that a combination of racial prejudice and poverty compelled their children to attend poor-quality, racially and economically segregated schools where they were drawn into the lifestyle and attitudes of oppositional culture. Because we focused on pre-school rather than high school, however, the immigrant parents in our focus groups discussed the possibility of losing control over their children more as a distant threat they hoped to be able to avoid than as a reality with which they were already coping.

Our multi-sited method allows us to highlight the crucial roles played by community context as well as culture in immigrant parents' concerns and strategies. Whereas immigrant parents at the Islamic School in Tempe were guardedly optimistic that they could shelter their children from what they viewed as the most negative elements of American society, West African, West Indian, and Latino immigrant parents in New York City expressed great concern about downward assimilation through their children developing adversarial attitudes; parents in Nuevo Campo, Arizona, were more concerned that their children would not be able to compete with native-born English speakers and with children growing up in more cosmopolitan settings.

GENDER DISTINCTIONS MADE BY IMMIGRANT PARENTS

A specific concern raised by Muslim parents in our focus groups was what they perceived as the hypersexualization of American society and therefore the need to practice and teach sexual modesty in the preschool. Some Muslim parents expressed a desire for even young children to be separated by gender because, as a mother from Egypt suggested, boys and girls are fundamentally different:

> We stress the values. What I found lacking at the public school my daughter was attending was a respect for the teacher, respect for the curriculum being taught. Shira was part of maybe twenty-five kids, one teacher. Has the public school ever thought of separating the two? Separating the boys so maybe they could have a different education, or better, because, you know, boys are different from girls, you know, because they have a different type of imaging that is in them as from the girls, maybe a separation?

Teachers at the Tempe Islamic School also emphasized the importance of teaching modesty:

INTERVIEWER: Do you talk with children about how girls should behave and how boys should behave?

TEACHER 1: Not behave, not exactly. But like the way they sit, the girls, you know? I show them to sit correctly for, uh, please, what is the word?

INTERVIEWER: Modesty?

TEACHER 1: Yes, you know, "Put your legs together."

TEACHER 2: I do the same thing with the girls. The boys are different, the way they sit, the way they talk. But the girl cannot lay on the floor. She's not allowed to. You know, this is my way.

TEACHER 3: Actually, one of the things I've noticed in public schools, and this is something that happened with a student, one of the girls. Her mother sent her to school in a dress, and on the playground a boy pulled up her dress. And actually even, as I see in public schools here, there are little girls, who they have their underwear exposed. We can explain it to them in a very gentle, calm way. But the main point is to talk to the mother. Just say, you know, "Can you put some shorts under there?" But the public preschools, I notice, they say, "Oh, it's just underwear. She's just a little girl." But for us, we take this, like, "This is your privacy."

Some Hispanic immigrant parents also expressed the desire for more gender segregation in their children's preschool. At a preschool in Tempe, while watching the video of a day in an Italian preschool that shows boys and girls together in the bathroom, a Mexican father stated emphatically that he did not think a unisex bathroom was appropriate: "I would not want my daughter to be in bathroom with boys. I would not put her in such a school." These comments are consistent with what Ramaswami Mahalingam (2006, 5–6) describes as new immigrants' "gender specific cultural ideals that valorize their women as more 'chaste' and 'family oriented' than White women." Two other Mexican fathers agreed that bathrooms should not be unisex. The mothers present said nothing. The teacher, herself an immigrant from Mexico some years earlier, was present during this discussion, which put her in an awkward position. After the session ended, she told us:

> When those fathers were talking about the bathroom, I didn't want to say anything. We have one bathroom in the classroom, and I tell children they should go in there one at a time and close the door. But some kids are scared to close the door, and at this age they are curious, so sometimes more than one goes in. I think the mothers are more aware of this than the fathers, because the mothers sometimes stay in the classroom. I didn't want to try to explain this because the fathers had such strong feelings about this.

Some scholars suggest that Latino fathers protecting the honor of their wives and daughters is an unattractive form of paternalistic machismo

(Mirande 1991), while others, who see the machismo label as a stereotypical view of Latino men (Harwood et al. 2002), argue that these Latino fathers are embracing the role of caring protector and provider (Mayo 1997).

Concerns expressed by immigrant parents about the need to safeguard
the modesty of their daughters were sometimes part of a larger pattern of
divergent concerns about their daughters and sons—as in this exchange
with a Sudanese mother in Iowa:

INTERVIEWER: When your children grow up, what do you hope they think
of themselves as? Americans? Sudanese? Sudanese Americans? American Sudanese?

MOTHER: American Muslim.

INTERVIEWER: So being Muslim is more important than being Sudanese?

MOTHER: For my son, I like it this way.

The qualification "for my son" suggests that this mother has different
identity concerns for her daughters. For her son, she values his identity as
Muslim over being Sudanese. By placing the term "American" before
"Muslim," she suggests that she also values her son's integration into
American society. She implies that her answer would be different with
regard to her daughters; perhaps she would place a higher value on her
daughters being Muslim and a lower value on their integration into American society. Such a gender distinction would be consistent with a long
history of immigrants to the United States making the pragmatic decision
to invest more heavily in their sons' preparation to function effectively in
the wider American society, while looking more to their daughters to preserve traditions of managing the home and raising children.

RELIGIOUS EDUCATION

Immigrant parents' selection of religious schools for their children can be
viewed not only as a reflection of piety but also, as Alejandro Portes and
Min Zhou (1993, 96) suggest, as a pragmatic solution to their "lack of opportunity of gaining access to middleclass white society, no matter how
acculturated they become. . . . Remaining securely ensconced in their coethnic community, under these circumstances, may be not a symptom of
escapism but the best strategy for capitalizing on otherwise unavailable
material and moral resources."

Statements made in our focus groups by immigrant parents about their
plans to send their children to religious schools and to shield them in other

ways as well from what they view as the deleterious values of their local community can be read as evidence of parents' ecological pragmatism, based on their calculations of the risks of exposing their young children to the values of the local community balanced against the costs and benefits of religious education and the building of ties among coreligionists. For example, in a focus group in Harlem, parents discussed options for Koranic education:

SENEGALESE MOTHER: My daughter is three years, and she already speaks English to me, like, "What are you talking about?" You know, when she doesn't know, or something. I'm troubled by that. I work a lot and do not have time to sit and teach her, and when I come and talk to her, all she speaks is English. So she doesn't know Arabic.

INTERVIEWER: How do you feel about that?

SENEGALESE MOTHER: I don't like that, but I don't have any alternative. I don't like at all, because I want her to learn Arabic and speak it and use it and all.

MALIAN MOTHER: I take my kids to the mosque.

IVORY COAST FATHER: They have school there every Saturday and Sunday, and we can bring them all day to make it easy for them. They don't know how to speak Arabic.

YEMENI FATHER: Another solution for this problem is to have our own school. I have a son in New Jersey who's ten years old, and he goes to Islamic school, supported or run by Egyptians and Pakistani people. But you have to pay—it's two hundred or three hundred dollars every month. So that's the solution, but it's kind of expensive. Nobody can afford that.

IVORY COAST FATHER: In Bergen it's three thousand dollars.

YEMENI FATHER: Three thousand!

IVORY COAST FATHER: Yeah, for one kid. With four kids, what can you do?

YEMENI FATHER: That's another problem!

Some immigrant parents enroll their children in religious schools with the hope that such an education will provide norms of conduct and protect their children from negative external community influences, as was expressed by preschool teachers at the Tempe Islamic School:

TEACHER 1: A big part of our religion is manners.

TEACHER 2: Manners.

TEACHER 1: So we encourage it. We practice it. The students see us practic-
ing. Part of Islamic studies is good manners. All the stories of the
prophets, and many parts of the Koran, you find talk about manners,
how to act in certain situations, how to act towards each other, how to
act towards parents, how to respect elders. I think that's a big part of
it as well.

TEACHER 3: We have clean language here. Our kids, we bring them here,
they're . . .

TEACHER 1: Innocent.

TEACHER 3: They're being built here. They graduate from here. If they go
to public school, they know, they get that personality. So that's why
we bring them here. To have the Islamic culture. It's good manners,
and nothing bad.

In Europe, conservative voices express a panicky fear about "Islamiza-
tion," a fear that Islamic immigrants bring with them beliefs that are anti-
thetical to the liberal, progressive, democratic, modern beliefs that Euro-
peans see as distinguishing themselves from the Islamic world (Balibar
2003; Guénif-Souilamas 2006). Such concerns are sometimes voiced in the
United States as well about Islamic immigrants, who are accused of holding backward views on women's rights and other social issues. But conservative social views tied to religion are hardly unique to religious Muslims. As we discuss later, in our focus groups some Mexican immigrant
parents also expressed concern about what they saw as the sexual immodesty of American society and the lack of religious values. And these concerns are shared by many socially conservative native-born Americans,
who, like many Muslim, Hispanic, and Korean immigrants, often enroll
their children in religious preschools.

ADULT AUTHORITY

In our focus group discussions, immigrant parents from a range of countries emphasized the importance of children having respect for adults and
of teachers as well as parents being authoritative figures in children's
lives. Many parents complained that their authority was undermined in
the United States by not being able to use corporal punishment with their
children. For example, in a focus group in Phoenix, a Mexican mother
said:

Children know that here, if you give a little spanking to your children, that
if someone hits them, then "Oh, I'm going to call the police because my mom

hit me." They are blackmailing their mother or father by saying, "I am going to tell the police on you because you hit me." Or she screams loud or something at the store and others give you a bad look, and this is not good either. That they take away the authority you have as a parent.

In our focus groups, immigrant parents not only from Mexico but also from South Asia, the West Indies, and the Middle East worried that the value they placed on a strict parenting style was not supported by American society. These concerns were raised, for example, in a focus group with West African parents in Harlem:

SENAGALESE FATHER: When you're from another country, it's a big conflict when you see how they do discipline here. We don't see anything wrong with a little spanking. Here, we are put in the position when we're raising our kids, not to touch them because they . . .

MALIAN MOTHER: If you even speak too loud, that's called verbal abuse.

SENEGALESE MOTHER AND TEACHING AIDE: And the kids know that. In my school, we say, "Keep quiet!" and the kids say back: "Don't raise your voice to me."

At this same site, a mother from Honduras who self-identified as Garifuna (black Caribbean) complained that raising children in the United States makes it difficult to instill values of respect because parents don't dare use physical punishment for fear of being reported for child abuse:

My older daughter is sixteen, and I can't handle her no more. I say to her: "God will take care of you. I can't handle you. I can't do nothing to you. I came to the United States to be somebody, to do something with my life, to have a better life. And I come here to sit in jail? Hell no! They've seen how we abuse the children, but they don't see how all the children abuse us. That has happened to me.

Mary Waters (1999, 220) heard similar stories from her West Indian immigrant informants in New York:

The parents we spoke with believe that physical punishment is the best way to deal with a child who has misbehaved. They are shocked that this is unacceptable in the United States, and consistently told us that it was one of the most disturbing aspects of living in this country. . . . That the state can dictate that a parent cannot beat a child is seen by these parents as a real threat to their ability to raise their children correctly.

Our informants, like Waters's informants, described feeling caught between following the parenting practices of their adopted country and holding on to their home culture's values and practices. Some expressed worry that their children's teachers, other authorities, and non-immigrant parents might perceive their approach to disciplining their children as confirmation of a stereotype of immigrants from their culture as harsh and ignorant. As a group of Sudanese mothers we interviewed in Iowa City explained:

MOTHER 1: I always tell my children, "We came here. This is a great country. But our country is great too. We have lots of very good values. We want you to keep the very good things about Sudanese culture. This country is great, but there is some stuff we don't agree with. We want you to get the best from this country, and the best from our country." I keep repeating this every time: "You are Sudanese," I tell them. "You are Sudanese."

MOTHER 2: Yeah, I'm very concerned, because they see us, we are different from the mainstream.

MOTHER 3: And our children are not sure. It's like we do very comprehensive work for them to get to the point where they are, what are they going to belong to. But the culture here is very strong. And also, we are not a big community here. They see the most educated people are Americans. The best speakers of English are Americans. The good things they see, the best houses, the best cars, the best education, everything good, belongs to Americans. And we are like the bottom of the society, so our children are confused. So I feel like we need to work hard to help them to find where they belong. I feel it is a very challenging job.

Robin Harwood and her colleagues (2002) suggest that Latino immigrant mothers of lower socioeconomic status (SES) attempt to compensate for their economic and social disadvantages by placing a greater emphasis in their parenting on "proper demeanor" than do higher-SES mothers. In discussing how the teachers deal with children's misbehavior in the video, some Mexican parents made a distinction between "enseñar" and "educar," both of which are usually translated into English as "to teach" but which in Spanish carry the related but distinct meanings of "to point out or show" (enseñar) versus "to raise or bring up" (educar) (Reese et al. 1995; Valdez 1996). Some Mexican parents suggested in our focus groups that the second responsibility—educar—and the raising of a child who is "una persona bien educada" is more their responsibility, as parents, than teachers' responsibility; therefore, intervention if their children misbehave at school should come from them more than from the teachers. One immigrant mother commented in a focus group: "In Mexico, teachers teach values, but they don't do that here in the U.S., so it is up to us."

Other researchers have made a parallel argument by emphasizing the cultural salience of the concept of "respeto," which can be translated from Spanish into English as "respect" but also carries a wider and deeper meaning, as Guadalupe Valdez (1996) demonstrated in her study of Mexican immigrant parents in south Texas. Harwood and her colleagues (2002, 25) define respeto as "proper demeanor," which involves, they suggest, "by definition, knowing the level of courtesy and decorum required in a given situation in relation to other people of a particular age, sex, and social status."

Valdez and Harwood locate respeto within a larger cultural mind-set that they suggest is more sociocentric and family-oriented than the value orientation of the larger society. This is consistent with Robert LeVine and Merry White's (1986) thesis that people moving from rural areas to cities within their country, as well as across national borders, bring their agrarian values and parenting styles with them, and that this leads to a disconnect between their educational expectations and those of the schools.

IDEALIZATION, MOURNING, AND NOSTALGIA

To counter feelings of inferiority, many immigrant parents idealize their home culture (Mahalingam 2006). Portes and Zhou (1993) suggest that for immigrant families living in cultural contact zones, an idealized cultural identity can serve as a buffer to the oppositional values of the surrounding community. We found evidence of this phenomenon, for example, in a Somali focus group at a community center in Iowa City, where a mother described how her community coped with the racism in the local community by claiming a sense of cultural superiority:

> You know, a lot of people, they don't like our color or something. It's just kids, but here some people, they do that. I want to know how my daughter is doing at the school, if she is doing good or not. There is a Somali staff person, she said, "Don't worry about problems our children have at the school. The people that come here from our country, they are smarter than the people here. So don't worry about your daughter."

Immigrant parents in several of the focus groups suggested that their home culture had more respect for cultural traditions and more patriotism:

INTERVIEWER: Some mothers have told me that they would like to see [Mexican] folk dances in school. Would you?

MOTHER 1: Yes, well, because in Mexico they organize festivals and the children dance.

MOTHER 2: They're graded for dancing!

MOTHER 1: It's a contest!

MOTHER 2: Part of a sports contest, with races, and everything.

MOTHER 3: In fact, here it seems that it is not so strong. They don't honor the flag. In Mexico the first thing they would do every Monday is to express honor to the flag.

MOTHER 4: Yes, every day they do it.

MOTHER 3: They have a color guard, right?

MOTHER 4: The principal talks on a microphone, and all the children start repeating along with him the national anthem. Here it's more different and shorter than in Mexico. In Mexico it is bigger.

Most immigrant parents saw no contradiction in encouraging in their children a patriotic identification with both their adopted country and their country of origin. As a father in Phoenix said in a focus group:

> Children should be taught to show respect for this country because this is where we are living. I tell my son to be proud of being Mexican and be proud of being American and show respect to both countries. We have both flags at our house, one for Fourth of July, the other for Cinco de Mayo. We need to celebrate our Mexican holidays so our children know who we are and feel proud of where they came from.

Idealization of the home country and culture is related to feelings of nostalgia and mourning that are characteristic of the psychodynamics of the immigrant experience (Henry, Stiles, and Biran 2005; Lijtmaer 2001; Yaglom 1993). We heard many expressions of nostalgia in our focus groups—for example, a Mexican mother in Iowa proudly claimed that all the food in Mexico is organic and fresh: "Here it is prepacked and not fresh. In Mexico everything is organic, everything has just been cut. You pull out the jicamas from the earth, and in the very same place you can eat them. Everything is different, the food is different."

We suggest that this comment can be read both literally, as a statement about food, and metaphorically, as an expression of an idealized version of the richness and authenticity of the culture left behind. As Salman

Akhtar (1999, 123) writes: "Nostalgia helps the immigrant defend against the aggression resulting from current frustrations."

Unfinished mourning for all that was lost in the experience of immigration, coupled with the stress of adjusting to the challenges of life in the new culture, can lead to raw emotions, as were expressed at the end of one of our focus groups in Mesa, Arizona. After we thanked the group and turned off our recording equipment, the discussion suddenly became heated. One mother who had argued during the session that Mexico should be given more credit for the strides it was making in education accused the other mothers of being too critical of Mexico and too enthusiastic about the United States. Several mothers responded that Mexico could not compare in education or in the opportunities available In the United States. One mother emotionally stated, "This country has done more for me than Mexico has ever done." In response, the Mexican patriot replied, "Of course we can't compare Mexico as it is now to where the United States is. But it is making strides. Don't be such Malinches [No sean tan Malinches]." The other women, insulted, angrily rejected this accusation.

Malinche is still remembered four centuries later for her complicity in the Spanish conquest of Mexico. The daughter of a noble Aztec family, Malinche was given to Hernán Cortés. She learned Spanish and served as an interpreter to Cortés, and she also bore him a son, Don Mahin Cortés, who is known as the first Mestizo. Malinche not only is regarded as the mother of the Mestizo race but has come to signify being a traitor and a harlot. As Cherríe Moraga (1994, 35) writes:

The sexual legacy passed down to the mexicana/Chicana is the legacy of betrayal, pivoting around the historical/mythical female figure of Malintzin Tenepal. As a Native woman and translator, strategic adviser and mistress to the Spanish conqueror of Mexico, Hernal Cortez, Malintzin is considered the mother of the mestizo people. But unlike La Virgen de Guadalupe, she is not revered as La Madre Sagrada, but rather slandered as . . . La Vendida, sell-out to the white race. Upon her shoulders rests the blame for the "bastardization" of the indigenous people of Mexico.

This history gives us a glimpse into the psychological and sociocultural complexity of the issues facing Mexican immigrant mothers. We can hear in the accusation "No sean tan Malinche" not only a call for immigrant mothers from Mexico to be loyal to Mexican culture, but also a concern about the cultural identity of their children. Mexican parents who move their families north and urge them to learn English and live among the Yanquis are vulnerable to accusations from their countrymen at home, from each other, and from themselves that they are reproducing Malinche's traitorous act, thereby producing an even more degraded, hybridized version of native Mexican-ness. If Malinche is the mother of the Mestizo race, immigrant Mexican mothers in the United States are the mothers of the new Mestizo—the "Mexican American."

We suggest that immigrant parents sometimes project their feelings of nostalgia and identification onto their feelings about their children's preschool. Immigrant parents' comments on what they want for their children in preschool and their judgments on their children's preschool experiences need to be interpreted in the context of their intense feelings about their move from their home country to the United States.

IDENTITY IN ENCLAVES AND CONTACT ZONES

The degree to which immigrants experience nostalgia and mourning for their country and culture of origin varies not just from individual to individual but also, we suggest, by the type of community in which they have settled. Immigrant parents who live in a community in the United States where most of the people they encounter in their daily life speak their language and share their culture have less reason to miss or idealize their country of origin than do immigrant parents who live in ethnic enclaves within a larger community, or in contact zones where immigrant and non-immigrant populations occupy the same space. Immigrant parents living in these different sorts of communities tend to have different concerns about cultural preservation and assimilation.

For example, as described in chapter 4, in our focus groups in Nuevo Campo, Arizona, parents expressed no concern about the danger of their children losing their Spanish-language fluency. These immigrant parents living along the border, unlike their counterparts in the enclave Mexican community in Mesa, did not heatedly debate their children's identity, nor did they idealize, denigrate, or mourn life in Mexico. For the Nuevo Campo parents, their Mexican heritage carried no negative connotations, led to few experiences of prejudice, and was not, in their view, at risk of being lost.

The focus group participants in Nuevo Campo expressed awareness that their location on the border with Mexico made their situation very different from that of immigrants living farther north. As one mother commented: "Being on the border has much relevance. It's different than up north." "North" is a relative term. In the Nuevo Campo focus groups, "north" sometimes was used to refer to Phoenix, but most often immigrant parents were referring to Yuma, a town twenty-five miles to the north, where about half of the population of 100,000 are of Mexican descent. For example, when we asked these parents if it was important for them to know English, the discussion began with a reference to Yuma and then turned to contrasting the advantages and disadvantages of life for Mexicans in Nuevo Campo versus farther north:

MOTHER 1: I speak English, but not as perfectly as my cousin in Yuma does. Since we're close to the border, since all our friends speak Spanish, that's why our English is not that good. If we go there [to Yuma], we are going to talk with people who speak English, and that's why there, they speak English, because they have friends who speak English, and we don't.

MOTHER 2: And in the stores.

MOTHER 3: We are pushed to learn it to go to the stores.

MOTHER 2: Not here that much, but when we go there, to Yuma.

MOTHER 4: They are farther from the border, and their classes are all in English. Since we are at the border, there are more children who come from Mexico, and their language, the first one, it's Spanish. And it's easier. I mean, we tend to be lazy: "I speak Spanish. Why should I speak English if they understand me anyway?"

These parents pointed out that the cultural and linguistic benefits of life as Mexican immigrants in Nuevo Campo needed to be balanced against the cost of more limited future opportunities for their children. These Nuevo Campo parents worry that their children would always lag behind those living in communities to the north in their acquisition of English and in their academic preparation. They also worry that it might be difficult for them to feel comfortable in the larger American society:

FATHER 1: When we took the children to play soccer against the kids in Yuma, they were kind of scared.

MOTHER 1: Our kids' English isn't as good. My older daughter, when we lived in Phoenix, her English was much better. But now that we came back to Nuevo Campo, it has become worse.

Life in Yuma and points farther north offers more opportunities compared to the life available to immigrants in Nuevo Campo. But a benefit of life on the border is that immigrants' children are growing up with a more secure sense of their Mexican culture and identity:

INTERVIEWER: Which other things are important to you? Which other things are important for maintaining your roots?

MOTHER 1: Traditions. In February, Flag Day. Cinco de Mayo. Mexico's history. Traditions we have.

INTERVIEWER: Does the preschool here do La Posadas [the Mexican Christmas ceremony] with the children?

MOTHER 5: Yes, here they do.

INTERVIEWER: And do you have folk dances ("bailables") here?

FATHER 1: Yes. We practice the folk dances a lot.

MOTHER 6: We have to pass those on to our children, but not here at the Head Start.

FATHER 1: The costumes. They dress them like "charritos" [traditional Mexican horsemen]. They dress them according to each one's tradition.

MOTHER 6: The colors of the Mexican flag. At the least, when there's Mexican Flag Day, in their classroom they should draw a Mexican flag, to color it and then to send it home or to display it there, so they know that that's flag day in Mexico.

MOTHER 2: All the traditions, a little of everything.

INTERVIEWER: And do your children feel Mexican? What do they call themselves?

MOTHER 3: My son says that he's Mexican American. My older girl, she feels Mexican at heart. She never says, "I'm from here." She says, "I'm Mexican, I'm Mexican." She doesn't say, "I'm from here, the United States."

The immigrant parents we interviewed who live in enclave communities face somewhat different challenges of culture, identity, and prejudice. Whereas children and their parents in Nuevo Campo, where everyone is Mexican, said they feel secure in their Mexican identity and free of prejudice unless they venture away from home—to Yuma or points beyond— immigrants living in enclave communities such as Mesa, Arizona, described facing different challenges, as did those living in contact zones, such as Riverdale, Iowa, and Harlem. In an "enclave community," by our definition, immigrant children attend a preschool where all or most of the students come from the same cultural background and where immigrant parents interact mostly with people from their own culture, in their home language, but surrounded by a wider non-immigrant community. We define "contact zones," in contrast, as settings where immigrant children attend preschools in which many of the children come from non-immigrant families and immigrant parents routinely interact with teachers, neighbors, and shopkeepers from both inside and outside their cultural group.

The parents we interviewed in enclave communities—such as the focus groups we conducted with Mexican parents in preschool programs in neighborhoods in and around Phoenix, where all of the children and a majority of the teachers were of Mexican origin—were generally pleased with their preschool's approach to incorporating cultural activities into the curriculum. For example, a Mexican mother in Mesa said that she was pleased that her child's preschool celebrated Mexican as well as U.S. holidays. In Queen Creek, a focus group of Mixtec-speaking parents in a preschool where about half of the children were Mixtec and half were Spanish-speaking Mexicans expressed appreciation that their Head Start program not only introduced their children to Mexican and American cultures, as well as to Spanish and English, but also was supportive of their Mixtec culture and language.

In contact zone communities, in contrast, immigrant parents expressed more anxiety about the degree to which they and their children would be welcomed and would find support for their cultural beliefs. In some of these contact zone communities, parents viewed their children's preschool as an oasis—a site where they found support for their culture that was lacking in the larger community. For example, at a community center near a public housing block in Iowa City, which is home to many recent immigrants from the Sudan, immigrant parents expressed general satisfaction that their children's preschool was adequately responsive to their concerns and reflective of their culture:

MOTHER 1: For me, I think it is very important for the school setting, to reflect part of my child's culture. Like if the school setting doesn't reflect any of my child's culture, my son will not feel like he belongs.

MOTHER 2: In Arabic, and numbers. When I used to work in the toddler room, I used to teach the kids to count from one to ten in Arabic. We have kids from different countries, who speak different languages at home, and they all count from one to ten. Most of them, even the American parents, are very happy about seeing the children counting from one to ten in Arabic. It is very important for the classroom to appreciate part of my child's culture.

Later in the discussion, some of these parents expressed concern about how things would change when their children moved from their community-run preschool to a public elementary school, where they would be in the minority. Unlike in Nuevo Campo, where children of immigrants from preschool through high school attend school alongside classmates who share their culture, Sudanese parents in Iowa City were well aware that their children would grow up in a world where they would be in the minority and that they would be likely to experience prejudice.

HYPHENATED AMERICANS?

Mexican immigrant parents identified themselves and their children using a variety of terms, none quite adequate to the complexity of their cultural in-betweenness:

INTERVIEWER: Your children, are they Mexicans or not?

FATHER 1: The roots. That's what's essential for them. The food. Everything.

INTERVIEWER: So how do they call themselves?

MOTHER 1: My child is four years old, and he, we lived in Mexico, we came here, and he didn't want to say he's from Mexico. He likes to say he's from the United States. He says that he likes the United States.

INTERVIEWER: Do all of you call yourselves Mexican? Is there anyone who calls himself Latino or Chicano?

MOTHER 2: Here they don't use the word "Chicano."

INTERVIEWER: What does Chicano mean to you?

FATHER 2: The one who is born here, born here and raised here.

MOTHER 2: From Mexican parents.

FATHER 1: Like they call it "Pocho."

INTERVIEWER: Do you like that term?

ALL: No.

INTERVIEWER: What do you want your children to call themselves?

MOTHER 3: My child was born here, and the older one, she says that she's from here, Mexican or American, Mingo, Minga.

INTERVIEWER: Pardon me?

MOTHER 3: Mingo, Mexican American.

For many U.S.-born people of Mexican heritage who identify themselves as Chicano, the term has a political dimension—an identification with an advocacy position for the political and economic rights and cultural uniqueness of Americans of Mexican origin. This dimension of "Chicano" is associated with Cesar Chavez and the farmworkers' strike, Chicana feminist authors such as Cherríe Moraga (1994) and Gloria Anzaldúa (1999), and musicians such as Richie Valens and Los Lobos (Montejano 1999). In contrast, for new immigrants from Mexico, the term "Chicano" generally lacks such positive and nuanced meanings and instead is used to distinguish people of Mexican heritage born in the United States from Mexican immigrants to the United States; the term also often has a negative connotation, as do the terms "Pocho" and "Cholo" (Matute-Bianchi 2008). For example, in Queen Creek, Arizona, newly arrived parents made it clear they were Mexicanos, not Chicanos:

INTERVIEWER: Do you think of yourselves as Mexicanos? Chicanos? Hispanos?

MOTHER 1: The Chicanos are born here. We are born there. The Hispanos are the ones speaking Spanish.

MOTHER 2: We are Mexicanos.

When we asked about the term "Chicano" in a focus group in Phoenix, a recently arrived Mexican immigrant mother replied: "We don't use that term here. They use that term in California." In Riverdale, Iowa, a mother answered our question "What are you?" by saying, "Mexicana." When we asked, "Not Chicana?" she replied, laughing, "No. We're not Chicanitos. I mean, they aren't from there or here. They're in Chicago." That she laughingly turned "Chicano" into the diminutive term "Chicanito" we take as a teasing put-down by a recent Mexican immigrant of earlier immigrants to the United States from Mexico who, she implied, had lost their Mexicanness and become rootless, belonging completely neither to here (the United States) nor there (Mexico). Her mention of Chicago may have been in part a pun on "Chicano" and in part a reflection of her attitude toward Mexicans living in Chicago in a Mexican community much larger and more settled than hers in a small town in Iowa. Her conflation of "Chicano" and "Chicago" we read as a mixture of envy toward and moral superiority over Mexicans, in Chicago and elsewhere, who have become more settled and hybrid in their identities. In speaking sarcastically about Chicano as an identity, this Mexican immigrant mother did not seem to consider the possibility that her U.S.-born children might grow up to embrace this label.

NO SOY DE AQUÍ O ALLÁ

Some of our informants found it difficult to label themselves or their children with a single identity term because they felt that they were in transition, having left one identity behind and not yet having secured another. Such feelings of being adrift were exacerbated by their experiences of racism and awareness of carrying a social stigma. In a focus group we conducted in Queen Creek at a Head Start program serving a migrant labor community adjoining a gated luxury housing development, parents referenced the character La India María, a creation of the actress, comedian, and film director María Elena Velasco. In one of her movies, La India María, an indigenous woman who comes from a rural mountain town and dresses in folkloric clothing, crosses the border to Houston to marry a Mexican American she calls "Mr. Pancho." In another movie, she moves to Los Angeles to work as a maid for a wealthy family, the Wilsons. In the Queen Creek discussion, parents suggested that their children's social standing was not even as high as that of La India María:

INTERVIEWER: How do you describe your children? They are what?

MOTHER 1: Gee, not even like "India María."

INTERVIEWER: Are they Hispanics?

MOTHER 1 AND MOTHER 2 (*laughing and singing*): Ni de aquí, ni de allá. (We're not from here nor there.)

MOTHER 2 (*holding out her hands to indicate half and half*): Ni de aquí, ni de allá.

MOTHER 3: Yes, they are not from here nor there, not from here, nor Mexico. We don't know where they are from.

Though their tone here was playful, these parents were expressing a heartfelt concern about their children's future identity and social status in the United States. In a film titled *Ni de aquí, ni de allá*, India María witnesses a murder at the Los Angeles airport and becomes a puzzle to the FBI agents who cannot determine whether she belongs in the United States or in Mexico. In the film, María's father tells her that if she leaves Mexico to go to the United States, the Americans will change her: "They are going to make you less than you are. You will then be 'neither from here nor there.'"

The phrase "ni de aquí, ni de allá" also came up in a focus group in an impoverished neighborhood in central Phoenix:

MOTHER 1: Yes, there are many racist people, especially here in Arizona.

MOTHER 2: Yes, especially here in Arizona. In Arizona there is a lot of racism, and it is sad. It is sad because you might say: "We are immigrants, so okay, you have the right to be upset because I am invading your property. But I am not stealing anything; I am working and I am earning what I eat." But our children are from here, so we can say: "You know what? This is their property too."

MOTHER 1: And *when* is it that we are from here?

MOTHER 2: *They* are from here.

MOTHER 3: We are not from here nor there.

MOTHER 1: Pretty soon, I won't be from here nor there

MOTHER 2: The most important thing is that we are here, in this country, to succeed, all of us.

MOTHER 3: And most of all, as long as we don't do anything bad here, to the government, if we don't steal from the government, if we are not harming anybody, the only reason why we are here is plain and simple: we came here to work and succeed and to go on.

Despite pervasive racism, these immigrant parents express determination to succeed in the United States and make a good future for their children. This was especially challenging for the immigrants living in Arizona in the era of anti-immigrant legislation coming out of the state legislature and Sheriff Joe Arpaio's raids on Mexican neighborhoods. These parents' comments suggest that they were well aware that they and their children were perceived as invaders (Santa Ana 2002) and as "takers," not "givers" (Murillo 2002). At the same time, however, these parents contest this labeling by emphasizing that they earn what they eat. They wonder if and when the day will come when society acknowledges that the United States belongs, if not to them, then to their children: "Our children are from here, so we can say: "You know what? This is their property too."

PREJUDICE AND THE SUFFERING OF THE IMMIGRANT

As researchers conducting a study on immigration and early childhood education, we were unsure what to do with the stories we heard in our focus groups from immigrant parents about prejudice they had encountered owing to their race, religion, country of origin, or suspected immigration status. Unless the parents were describing incidents in which they or their children were treated unfairly at preschool, these stories at first struck us as off-topic. We eventually came to the conclusion, however, that if our informants considered it important for us to hear about these incidents, it was our obligation to listen carefully to what they were saying and then respond in some way.

We were struck by the parallel between our initial reaction to these stories told by immigrant parents in our focus groups and what preschool teachers told us about sometimes feeling overwhelmed by the poverty and experiences of prejudice suffered by the children in their classrooms and their families. As the director of a preschool in Phoenix said to us:

> I know, of course, how difficult the lives are of my students and their families. We do what we can. For instance, we ask local businesspeople to donate Christmas presents each year, because it breaks our hearts to know that many of our children's families can't afford to buy them anything. And we hear stories about them losing their apartments and not being able to find work and of being the victims of crime and violence and discrimination. But I have to remind my teachers that there is only so much we can do. We help as much as we can, making referrals to government aid programs and to private social services programs like Chicanos Por La Causa and the Community Food Bank. But we have to focus on what we know how to do best, which is early childhood education and advising parents on child development, like reading to their children. If my teachers don't focus on those things we *can* do for them, there's a danger of them burning out.

Just as teachers must deal every day with the impacts of poverty and prejudice on the lives of their students and their families, so must we researchers who study early schooling move beyond considerations of curriculum, pedagogy, and provision and explore the impacts of poverty and prejudice on how immigrant parents view their children's preschools. Our study shows that the suffering many new immigrants experience in their lives in the larger society infuses their attitudes toward their children's preschool, leading some to look to the preschool as an oasis of support and others to see the preschool as just one more site where they and their children are misunderstood and even at times ill treated.

The situation was fraught in a New York City contact zone where we conducted interviews. At a church preschool in Harlem that serves a mixture of African American, African, and Caribbean families, a group comprising the African American teachers and the director, who was born in Senegal and educated in the United States, described some tensions between the immigrant and native-born communities they served:

INTERVIEWER: Is there any tension that you ever see among the different cultural groups?

TEACHER 1: A child will call another child a name.

TEACHER 2: Don't you think they are repeating, though, what they've heard?

TEACHER 1: Sure, but still, it feels the same for a child who is at the receiving end of it.

INTERVIEWER: So you are saying that sometimes kids from Africa . . .

TEACHER 1: Oh yeah, quite often, not just sometimes.

INTERVIEWER: What do kids say?

TEACHER 2: Kids only absorb what adults around will say or do. And you can tell it is an adult that is leading them to say: "I'm not playing with you because you're from Africa."

TEACHER 1: That sounds familiar.

INTERVIEWER: Coming from a child who is . . .

TEACHER 3: African American.

INTERVIEWER: So you suspect that it's reflecting what they're hearing at home?

DIRECTOR: Definitely. I don't think kids could make it up. Between Hispanic and African families, and between African American and African parents, I don't perceive any, you know, any kind of, uh, interaction. And you know, it's hard for people also to acknowledge it. We did a big workshop about it at the beginning of the school year, to see how we're going to handle it.

INTERVIEWER: It goes both ways?

DIRECTOR: For adults, yes, well of course, it goes both ways.

INTERVIEWER: Do you get African immigrant kids critical of African Americans?

TEACHER 3: It's more the other direction.

TEACHER 2: They're the newest kid on the block.

INTERVIEWER: I don't know what I was expecting. Maybe I thought, because you have an Afrocentric curriculum and ideals, maybe there'd be more of a sense of connection between the African Americans and the African immigrants.

TEACHER 3: Maybe with the most educated among us.

It does, indeed, go both ways. In our focus group with parents at this preschool, some immigrant parents, as quoted earlier, criticized the values reflected in aspects of African American culture and more generally in American culture.

Studies by Nancy Foner and others suggest that such tensions between

African Americans and immigrants from Africa and the Caribbean are not unusual. As Foner (2005, 42) writes about West Indians in New York City:

> Immigrants often seek to distance themselves from African Americans and Puerto Ricans as a way to avoid the stigma associated with these groups. Much has been written about West Indians' attempts to assert an ethnic identity—in terms of country of origin or as West Indian—in order to make a case that they are culturally different from and superior to African Americans.

We found tensions between new and more settled immigrant communities in our other contact zone settings as well. In an Arizona preschool serving new immigrants from Mexico as well as native-born Mexicans, we heard complaints from the new immigrants about the earlier immigrants:

INTERVIEWER: Do you get much help from the Mexican parents who have been here longer?

MOTHER 1: No, not much. Ms. Maria and Ms. Juana [*the classroom teachers*] help us.

MOTHER 2: The ones here longer, the Chicanos, they don't talk to us much.

In another focus group, a teacher gave us some insight into this dynamic:

INTERVIEWER: In some other focus groups, we were surprised to hear from new immigrants that the older Hispanic communities, second-, third-, fourth-generation, have actually not helped. We were surprised because we thought that they would be the ones helping, and being like a bridge between the cultures.

TEACHER: No, they worked so hard to acclimate themselves and to fit into the community that they don't want to be like pulled away and be associated with the new people coming in.

We were surprised to hear that our Islamic informants in Phoenix had little experience with prejudice:

INTERVIEWER: Do you or your kids ever run into prejudice?

EGYPTIAN FATHER: No, people are very nice to us. In our neighborhood, people go out of their way to be kind.

PAKISTANI MOTHER: When I am out in public, dressed like this [*in a long dress and head scarf*] I, if anything, I am treated with respect, maybe more than if I dressed like Americans. Like men hold doors for me when I go to the store.

PAKISTANI FATHER: Maybe you heard that right after 9/11 a Sikh taxi driver was stabbed in Mesa? The attacker thought he was Muslim. But that was a very rare thing.

Somali mothers in Iowa City, in contrast, reported more experiences with being treated rudely, stared at, and sometimes confronted about their beliefs. This may happen to the Somali mothers more often than it does to the Islamic School mothers in Phoenix because they are not only Muslim but also black and poor, and more covered up and dressed in darker clothes when they go out in public. In Harlem, West African Islamic parents complained, not of being stared at, but of being viewed by the black Americans in their community as "FOBs" (fresh off the boat) who are insufficiently Americanized and perceived as hostile to their local community.

One explanation for the differences we find from community to community in new immigrants' reports of encountering prejudice is that in each community a different racial, cultural, or ethnic group takes on the burden of the role of the stigmatized other on whom the anxieties and frustrations of the larger community are projected. In a city such as Phoenix, where Islamic immigrants make up a relatively small percentage of immigrants and of the total population and Mexicans, for historical, economic, and political reasons, are the go-to scapegoat, Muslims are unlikely to encounter prejudice. In a small town such as Riverdale, Iowa, where just about all of the immigrants are from Mexico and there is deep ambivalence about the town and school having rapidly shifted from being almost all white to being half-Mexican, it is not surprising that Mexicans report encountering prejudice.

In the focus group with parents in the homogeneous border town of Nuevo Campo, we heard no complaints from the parents or their children, either at the preschool or in the wider community, about encountering prejudice. In enclave communities, such as those in central Phoenix where most of the children and the teachers were Spanish-speaking immigrants from Mexico, parents had no complaints about prejudice at their children's preschool, but many stories of prejudice in the wider community. In contact zone settings, such as the preschools in Harlem and Riverdale, Iowa, immigrant parents and teachers reported tensions both in the preschool and in the wider community.

Some immigrant parents reported that they had been accused of being in the country illegally and were therefore unwelcome. For instance, a Mexican mother in a Mesa, Arizona, focus group reported this incident:

I was buying groceries, and an American woman said, "What are you doing here? This store is not for you. Do you have one of these?" And she showed me a driver's license. "If you don't have one of these, you don't have any right to buy here. Go away!" This time I was with my son. He was scared, saying, "What is that woman yelling, Mom?" I didn't reply to the woman. Nobody helped me, not even the manager. The store manager could have talked to her, asked her to calm down, but he didn't say anything. Nobody did anything, and the lady kept yelling. That was the most difficult experience I have felt here, where the racism showed through.

Another member of this focus group contributed a similar story:

One time my friend and I were taking our children to the doctor, and we were in the taxi, and the driver was bothering us. He was saying that we should go back to our country, that we didn't have any right to be here, that we were using what is only for citizens. Things like that. And since he was so upset, I was scared. I said to my friend, "We are two women, with two babies, and if he wants to do something bad, he can hurt us." He was so upset, and yes, so racist.

In a focus group in Phoenix, a Mexican father who does drywall and plaster work described feeling stared at when he went shopping where the "American people" shopped:

I'm a finisher. When I come from my work, I'm covered with cement dust. I'm dirty, and since I'm Latino, I usually go to Food City, because that is where the Latinos go. We go to different places. So this time I go to Fry's, where the American people go, and I see the difference. They look at me, so clean, and me so dirty, buying chicken. I feel they are staring at me.

This speaker did not allude directly to his immigration status, or suggest that he was looked down upon by middle-class customers at Fry's because they suspected him of being undocumented. However, his binary description—they were "so clean" and he was "so dirty"—mirrors the discourse of disgust and contamination that, as Otto Santa Ana (2002) argues, provides the dominant metaphors in the larger culture for the threat of being overwhelmed by a "brown tide" coming from below the border. This man's story was one of transgression, of being in a place where he did not belong, a place he was accused of contaminating with his presence.

We assume that some of the informants in our focus groups were undocumented. We do not know for sure because their children's preschool programs did not ask about immigration status, and neither did we. The specter of racist policing and draconian legislation in Arizona explains why so many of the stories of discrimination were recounted by immigrant parents in focus groups in that state. But these accounts were by no means limited to Arizona. In Tennessee, immigrant parents also shared stories of marginalization and unfair practices associated with their identity. One mother explained, for example, that her nephews were kicked off their school bus because "they're Hispanic":

> I have two nephews, and the bus driver stopped, and because they're Hispanics, and she made them get off. And then, the next day they had to talk to the principal because the driver didn't take them home, but she made them get off in the street, because, supposedly there were others, black ones who were fighting, and according to her, everybody was fighting. And she made them get off in a street. She left them there. Then my nephews had to walk home. Then, I think that there really is racism or favoritism.

In our interviews with teachers and other staff members, participants sometimes made comments that confirmed the immigrant parents' concerns about being stereotyped. For example, at the end of one teacher focus group, a white Anglo teacher turned to us to praise one of her students who walked by, the son of immigrant parents. She remarked on his clean demeanor and good looks, stating: "He is so polite, you put a tuxedo on him, and he could be a waiter at the White House."

In Riverdale, Mexican parents told us how unwelcome they felt when they shopped in the nearby town of Muscatine:

INTERVIEWER: How do you think the other people see Hispanics here?

MOTHER 1: When I go to Muscatine, there are so many white people there, and they look at us like I shouldn't be there. Because we speak Spanish.

MOTHER 2: Like when we go to Walmart in Muscatine, there are people there, there's a woman there who told me that we should go back to Mexico.

MOTHER 3: But of all the people, there are just a few, there are many Americans who are very respectful and speak to you nicely.

MOTHER 1: Yes, but I had once a lady who, like that [*makes a rude gesture*]. She did.

MOTHER 2: Here in Riverdale it's peaceful. Nobody bothers you. Well, that's what I think. But when I go to Muscatine, I take my husband because I'm scared, because there are not many people like us, only a few. The majority there in Muscatine are just like that lady I ran into in the store.

But not everyone in this focus group agreed that is peaceful in Riverdale:

INTERVIEWER: And what about in Riverdale? Any problems here?

MOTHER 4: Lately, I have had several conflicts. There have been people who have lived here, and they say, they have shown up to throw things at my door. Like to say, "No, we don't want you here." Here on the doorknob, they put something nasty and something that smells like gas or something like that.

In our focus group discussion with the preschool teachers in Riverdale, we were given more insight into the nature of tensions between the old Anglo and new Hispanic communities:

TEACHER 1: There's this committee in town. The purpose of this committee is to bring everyone together.

TEACHER 2: It's usually just this big, huge town celebration on Saturday in May. This year it was like an alternative to Cinco de Mayo. They actually had it. It was like a three-day festival for the Midwest or something.

These comments refer to a nativist response to the Mexican newcomers' Independence Day celebration, a response organized, ironically, by a committee that was supposed "to bring everyone together."

Rawer feelings came out at the end of a discussion with a group of teacher's aides who had grown up in Riverdale:

AIDE 1: The whole Spanish pride thing is huge. The people will have the Spanish flag or the American flag. It's like they want to come here so bad and have a better life, but they're not going to leave their Spanish heritage. It's almost like they resent the United States. They resent their opportunities here, but they're here.

AIDE 2: There's a reason why you're here. Because if you go back to Mexico, you're not going to get $500 a week.

AIDE 3: I hate to sound mad, but I think the town is a lot dirtier now. People don't take care of their houses.

AIDE 2: Or the yards . . .

AIDE 3: But they drive nice cars.

AIDE 1: And we used to walk around all the time. We'd go and sit down in town . . .

AIDE 2 (*laughing*): . . . in our cheerleading outfits! Now it's like, "Put some jeans on!" I mean, it's just, you don't know the people, even though you are in the same community, you don't know the people.

INTERVIEWER: Are all the community leaders white still?

AIDE 3: Yes. They're doing a good job. They're trying to do it. But it's like they try to recognize the Hispanic culture and then they have the white culture. They're not doing enough together. But I don't think people here want that.

AIDE 1: I don't think either side wants to mix.

AIDE 2: Hispanics aren't ready, seriously. The majority of Hispanics aren't ready to make change.

AIDE 3: Kids are, the young kids.

AIDE 1: I wish they would take care of their lawns and that they would not play the loud music all the time. It's one of those hidden rules that needs to get across. It's not just the laws. It's like the hidden rules of the community.

AIDE 3: Yeah, it's kind of like, "We're here. This is our house."

AIDE 2: "And we're not changing!"

AIDE 3: Like, "Don't do that!" The backwards parking downtown. You don't do that in this town.

AIDE 1: Like you need to give them the paper when they move in: "Here are the rules."

AIDE 2: First day of school, you would think they would just catch on, or know better.

AIDE 1: And we mow our lawns here.

AIDE 3: But then it's kind of a poor white thing too, you know? Because they don't necessarily take care of their yards either.

Compared to these comments by the teacher's aides, statements by River-dale teachers were more sympathetic to the immigrant community, more nuanced, and more ambivalent, and they conveyed a sense of responsibility and regret. In a focus group we conducted on a return visit to Riverdale, the Anglo preschool teachers described feeling caught sometimes between their desire to help the immigrant families whose children they taught, on the one hand, and their location on the other side of the Anglo-Mexican divide in the town, on the other:

TEACHER 1: I live in this community, and a lot of the times, you know, from my relatives and neighbors, there's always this, "What are you doing at that school? If they're here, then they should be speaking English." It's frustrating. But yet we do have a community group now that's trying to get the word out there about culture, and the town is very open to that. Every May we have a big celebration here, a big cultural festival. The town's very willing and open to that. And like these people that say like, "What are you doing there?" They're the ones going down to the stores and eating the tacos and the rice and enjoying all that. They're enjoying the culture, so it can be frustrating.

INTERVIEWER: Is the community kind of freaking out because it's not looking like their town anymore?

TEACHER 2: Have you had a chance to drive through downtown at all?

INTERVIEWER: Yes, we had lunch there.

TEACHER 3: And the majority of the stores downtown are Hispanic.

INTERVIEWER: We had a great meal.

TEACHER 2: Yeah, the food is wonderful.

INTERVIEWER: But the community generally is struggling?

TEACHER 1: I don't know what it is anymore.

TEACHER 3: I think things are better now. Just because the teaching now is being done in English [after the bilingual program was discontinued]. But yet, I think you'll always just have those, you know, I wouldn't call them the grandmas and grandpas. It's just that age, that cultural, you know, "Well, when I was young, blah, blah, blah." You know. Times change, and you find that anywhere, I think, anywhere you go.

TEACHER 4: Sometimes it gives me these mixed feelings like, "Ugh, all right, I know they'll learn English. You know, I know it's going to come." Or: "Darn it. You know it. Speak English!" My feelings go back and forth. "You know English. So why aren't you using it?"

Teacher 1 in this exchange described catching herself making stereotypical assumptions:

This happened last year. The Presbyterian church here, we had a Spanish-speaking man come up wanting to come to church, needing to talk to somebody and wanting to come to church. And my church is all white, no Spanish. I was the only one that could speak Spanish with him, and I kept referring him to the Catholic church: "You know, down the street. It's ten o'clock, ten o'clock. You'll make it, you'll make it." He was, "No, no Catholic," very adamant about not going to that Catholic Church. I just thought, *Well, I know there's a Spanish service at the Catholic church,* and then it was like, oh, a big eye-opener for me. Yeah.

This teacher came to realize that her preconception that "whites" attend Presbyterian services and "Spanish" attend Catholic services was constraining her understanding of this man's needs. At the same time, however, her conflation of race and language suggests another blind spot. She used the term "Spanish," which is a word for a language, in contrast to the term "white," which is used to convey race. She reduced immigrant group members to a language juxtaposed with a group reduced to its race (Adair forthcoming).

Teacher stereotypes about immigrant families also have a more direct effect on young children's education in the form of the tyranny of low expectations and self-fulfilling prophecies (Adair 2012). Kevin Swick (2004) argues that teachers who hold the (erroneous) belief that Mexican parents place little value on education and are not interested in being involved in their children's school tend to drive these parents away. Mariana Souto-Manning (2007) argues that teachers who view the children of Mexican immigrants as being at risk for academic failure make such failure more likely by applying a deficit perspective and being too quick to put these children in remediation programs. Some immigrant parents who are aware of the risk from the self-fulfilling prophecies of their children's teachers use strategies such as enrolling their children with Anglo given names. In her case study, Souto-Manning (2007, 402) describes Esperanza, a Mexican mother who registered her five-year-old son Idelbrando in school under the name Tommy:

So that no one would know he is Mexican. So that he would have a better chance to be successful in school than his brothers. . . . By giving Idelbrando a new name, Esperanza sought to spare him from such linguistic and cultural stereotypes that might hinder his schooling experience. She had seen it happen twice, with Nicolas and Antonio. She didn't want to see it happen again.

DEFERENCE

Mexican immigrants in our focus groups in Riverdale, Iowa, and else-where reported that their response to both explicit prejudice and the expe-rience of being underestimated, stereotyped, and misunderstood was not outright anger so much as disappointment mixed with resignation. The complexity of their reactions is captured in the verb "agachar" (to crouch, hunker down, or bow down); immigrant parents in several of our focus groups used this word, which was also a central theme, even when the word itself was not used, in many other discussions. Bowing down is con-sistent with a communal or family-oriented perspective ("familismo") that discourages individual assertiveness at the expense of the group.

Such a stance of lying low is a pragmatic tactic in a setting where raids in search of undocumented workers are commonplace and public support for anti-immigration legislation is growing. On the other hand, the notion of deferring to prejudice can also be taken as a symptom of the shame of long experiences of asymmetrical relationships between Mexico and the United States and between Mexicans and Americans, as was expressed in a discussion in Phoenix:

MOTHER 1: In Mexico—I'm going to talk about my country since the ma-jority here are Mexican—in Mexico they make us think Americans are a superior race, and when you are here you realize that we are the same.

MOTHER 2: Hispanics are even better.

MOTHER 1: There are poor and rich, people who study and people who don't, people who have good jobs and people who don't. I mean, we are equal. But they make us think in that way, so the ones who come here, we come here frightened.

MOTHER 2: With our heads lowered [*"agachaditos"*].

MOTHER 3: And people say: "Don't speak so loud. They are going to hit me." Then you realize, "Hey, I am equal to them."

Some immigrant parents were pained to see their children take such a stance of deference at preschool:

At the school, sometimes the teachers tell something to my children, and because they don't know what they are saying, they bend their heads [*"agachar"*] and don't answer. Because they are just learning English, that's why they don't know many of the things the teachers are saying. For exam-ple, yesterday my daughter wet herself because she did not know how to ask permission to go out. Even though the other teacher [*who speaks Spanish*] was there, my daughter was shy because she doesn't speak the language.

Immigrant parents who might reluctantly accept the pragmatic need to hunker down themselves and at least pretend to be deferential at work expressed a desire to see their children stand up to prejudice at school:

> I have a daughter who had a problem: a boy was disrespectful to her. He told her she was a Mexican, as an insult. Then my daughter felt bad, but since I have always told her, "You don't have to lower your head [*"agachar"*], and whoever it is, you have to stand up, to resist. Be polite and answer with intelligence." She told him: "I'm not from here, but I feel like I am from here, because I have studied here since I was a girl. And I am more intelligent than you in that regard because I am educated. My parents have educated me, something you don't have."

What this mother implied was that her daughter had "educación" and her assailant did not. As Sofia Villenas (2002) explains, having "una buena educación" means being respectful and having good manners, moral values, loyalty to the family, and religious faith.

THE ROLE OF BICULTURAL STAFF

At the preschools where we conducted interviews that had a sizable number of children from one culture and language group, there was usually at least one teaching assistant who was herself a recent immigrant. At a preschool on the Upper West Side in New York, teachers and teacher's aides who were themselves immigrants from Mexico, Central America, and the Spanish Caribbean told us that most public preschools now have staff members who are bilingual and bicultural:

> Here in Manhattan most of the schools are changing. If you go to a public preschool, you see that there are always Hispanic mothers, and there's always a head teacher who, you know, looks like you [*nodding toward the blond interviewer, Jennifer Adair*], you know, Anglo-Saxon. But there's always also an assistant teacher who is like us. The system is changing a lot. Before, when my daughter was in preschool, it was different, but now, there's always a teacher who is Hispanic, and there's more involvement of parents.

Another teacher, who had migrated from the Dominican Republic twenty years earlier and whose children had attended the program, told us that when she first came to the school as a parent aide, there was a pervasive sense that immigrant staff members were disempowered and their cultures unappreciated: "They were changing our names in those days. Maria was called Mary, and Josefina was called Josephine. So that was where the frustration was coming from. Now there's more 'concientizacion' ['critical consciousness']." (This term is associated with Paolo Freire [1974] and his writings on organic processes of community empowerment.)

In our focus group interviews, both immigrant parents and non-immigrant teachers expressed appreciation for bicultural, bilingual staff members as cultural guides, translators, and mediators. However, some comments made in these interviews also suggested that neither immigrant parents nor non-immigrant teachers appreciate the difficulties faced by the bicultural staff members in their programs as they struggle to negotiate their in-between positionality. In our focus groups, teachers who were themselves immigrants discussed both the role they play as cultural and language translators and mediators and the difficulties they encounter in situations where they felt pressured to speak as either the voice of their community or the voice of the program. Both immigrant parents and non-immigrant school staff look to bicultural, bilingual staff members to provide a bridge between the worlds of home and school (Monzó and Rueda 2008), but both sides tend to underestimate the complexity of this task (Adair, Tobin, and Arzubiaga 2012; Lucero 2010; Rueda, Monzó, and Higareda 2004).

In the course of becoming professional early childhood educators, immigrant teachers must renounce positions they held before joining the field and adopt the field's central beliefs—for example, a belief in the efficacy of play and constructivism. If immigrant teachers too completely adopt the positions of their non-immigrant fellow teachers, however, they risk being seen as alienated from their culture of origin, or worse, as a traitor to their community.

To avoid being criticized by either or both sides, bicultural teachers at times present themselves differently to their colleagues and to immigrant parents. Immigrant teachers in our focus groups reported not only code-switching in their conversations—speaking Spanish, for example, with parents and English with their monolingual colleagues—but also changing their speech register and demeanor and even presenting differently nuanced versions of their own beliefs, in concert with those of their interlocutors. Some bicultural, bilingual teachers reported in the focus group discussions that when asked to translate in conversations between parents and other staff members—as they often are asked to do—they do some editing of what is said to avoid exacerbating tensions by making the two sides more aware of how differently they see things.

In Riverdale, Iowa, the only bilingual, bicultural staff member at the preschool and elementary school was Elisa, the family support worker, who communicated with immigrant families and translated between parents and teachers. The teachers told us about Elisa during a conversation in which they recounted their struggles to communicate with the Spanish-speaking parents:

INTERVIEWER: When you do home visits, do you bring an interpreter?

TEACHER 1: It depends on how comfortable I am with that family. Sometimes I will go by myself, and other times, if it's something really important, I'll take Elisa, the family contact person.

INTERVIEWER: Do you feel like parents rely on you for help with English things, or things in the community or the town?

TEACHER 2: We're very fortunate that we have Elisa, our family contact person. She's wonderful working with our families.

The teachers viewed Elisa as a valuable member of the school staff whose key contributions were translating during parent-teacher discussions and helping the Mexican immigrant community adjust to life in a small Iowa town. When we interviewed Elisa, she explained that her main role is to help the parents feel comfortable at the school and to better understand how school works. One of the ways she does this is not only to translate for teachers but also to expand their explanations to make them more culturally understandable to parents, to whom she often offers more detailed explanations of terms and concepts in her translation than were originally present in what the teachers said.

In our focus groups, teachers who were themselves immigrants tended to be careful about either criticizing or endorsing the approach to teaching shown in our U.S. video. However, when these immigrant teachers watched and discussed the videos we showed of French and Italian preschools, their responses tended to be livelier and less guarded. We speculate that the task of watching videos of preschools in other countries unleashed more complicated and ambivalent reflections and reactions than did the task of watching a film about a U.S. preschool that showed progressive practices they were familiar with and that produced expected comments and reactions, largely in line with those of their non-immigrant colleagues.

For example, at a preschool in New York City a group of Spanish-speaking, mostly immigrant teachers (eight of the nine teachers were from Mexico or the Dominican Republic) watched and then discussed our video showing a day in a French "école maternelle" (the French term for "kindergarten"). These teachers expressed surprise that a single teacher in France was expected to teach a class of twenty-five students, and they were critical of what they saw as a lack of adequate supervision of children on the playground. We were accustomed to the French video provoking such expressions of concern and disapproval among native-born U.S. teachers. But in this focus group with immigrant teachers, the discussion took an unexpected turn. The discussion began predictably enough with a teacher saying that it was awful how children could fight without a teacher intervening: "At recess, they were killing each other, and nobody went to break it up." Another teacher changed the topic, faulting the French teacher for being too rushed in her interactions with immigrant children: "I mean, sorry, but, Oh my God! I didn't like it when the teacher didn't give the boy a chance to answer the questions she was asking." A third teacher added that they even let the children use knives during mealtime: "The knife and the fork for the children. It's not suitable for three-year-old children." It was at this point that the conversation took an unexpected turn, as the teachers debated the wisdom and appropriateness of children being allowed to use knives in preschool. One teacher acknowledged the truth that "real" knives would not be found in U.S. preschools, but she wondered aloud, "Why not?" and observed that young children were allowed to use knives to cut their food in many homes. This led to a spirited discussion about the cultural nature of assumptions about children's capabilities:

TEACHER 1: I think that it can be the influence of the culture. I mean if they can handle it.

TEACHER 2: Many people teach the children at an early age to use knives.

TEACHER 1: But, that's what I'm telling you. Her hands were not used to holding a knife.

TEACHER 3: The one who was cutting the meat. She didn't have . . .

TEACHER 1: She didn't feel comfortable.

TEACHER 4: It [*the use of knives by the children*] was okay. But maybe we are looking at this in the wrong way. I think by watching the video, I question ourselves. I have walked in the shoes of somebody who we say about them: "They don't understand us." Because by watching that video, we are like the Americans to our children. What I mean is, remember that in our native country there are seven-year-old children who cook; there are children who can take care of other children. They have skills.

In this conversation, we see immigrant teachers drawing on their memories and experiences prior to emigrating to the United States to challenge the taken-for-grantedness of middle-class American beliefs about what children are capable of doing. Teacher 4 accuses her colleagues of having too limited a view of children's potential, in the same way that Anglo teachers underestimate the abilities of their immigrant students. In her criticism, we hear a form of cultural critique: she suggests that immigrant children come to school with knowledge and abilities that are underestimated or, worse, considered dangerous by teachers who view them through a U.S. professional lens. Her comment, "We are like the Americans to our children," is less an accusation than a realization, or even an epiphany. This exchange was one of the rare instances in our study when immigrant teachers directly challenged U.S. early childhood educational beliefs and practices. In her epiphanic declaration, Teacher 4 names the problem that she and the other immigrant teachers suffer from as a forgetting of things they once knew, and worse, this is a forgetting that makes them view their own children through foreign eyes, to look at them in terms of their deficits rather than their strengths.

The argument put forward by these teachers is consistent with anthropological studies of childhood that challenge ethnocentric Western ideas about normative child development and expand our notions of the capabilities of young children (LeVine and White 1986; Rogoff 2003; Whiting and Edwards 1988). Research shows the value of preschools employing culturally responsive approaches to children and families from diverse backgrounds (De Gaetano, Williams, and Volk 1998; Goodwin 2002; Graue 2005; Souto-Manning 2007). For non-immigrant and white middle-class teachers, such culturally situated, responsive approaches require new learning. What is required for immigrant teachers is not just new learning but also a not forgetting.

CONCLUSION

In discussions of identity, immigrant parents mix idealism with a pragmatism that reflected their assessment of the opportunities and constraints of the communities in which they had settled. Resisting the negative features of American culture is a more pressing task for parents living in contact zone communities, where they and their children experience prejudice, than in enclave communities, where their contact with outsiders is more limited (Cornfield and Arzubiaga 2004).

Immigrant parents who believe that their children's preschool is not providing a complete education—meaning an education that includes moral teaching—attempt to address this gap by ramping up their moral education at home or enrolling their children in a religious school. Concern about the hypersexuality and gender immodesty of American society is another reason parents chose church- or mosque-based preschools. Immigrant parents who believe in the value of corporal punishment feel undermined by prohibitions in the United States on spanking their children and are afraid of being reported to child protective services; they also feel humiliated and angered by their sense that both their children's teachers and the wider society view them as ignorant and cruel.

In many of our focus groups, the discussions shifted from talk about preschool to stories about discrimination experienced by immigrant parents and their children in the wider society. These stories were more common in contact zones, where immigrant and non-immigrant populations occupied the same, sometimes contested space. In these settings, immigrants were also more likely to idealize the values and associated identities of their country of origin. Immigrants also reported using the strategies of being deferential and lying low to get by.

Immigrant parents' and their children's teachers often have different views of who is to blame for misunderstandings and tension between the immigrant and receiving communities. Bicultural staff members struggle to balance their loyalty to their community of origin with their professional role and to integrate their cultural understanding with their professional knowledge.

Chapter 6 | Facilitating Dialogue

As THE FOCUS GROUP STAGE of our project drew to a close, we returned to Riverdale, Iowa, for a follow-up session with a mixed group of teachers and immigrant parents. Up to this point in the project, all of our focus group discussions had been with parents *or* teachers. An interpreter was present to interpret between the English-speaking teachers and Spanish-speaking parents. A teacher began the session by thanking the parents for coming, letting them know that the staff at the preschool was eager to get to know them better, and that their goal was to help young children feel comfortable at their school. The teachers then listened as several Mexican parents described difficulties they were having in town and with the school. They gave examples of discrimination they had encountered and of their economic struggles. They expressed sadness that the bilingual program in the preschool had been cut, and frustration that they were not able to attend meetings at school scheduled during their work time. When the parents finished speaking, one of the teachers, with a tone of exasperation, asked: "If it is so hard here, then why are you here? Why don't you go back to Mexico?" The parents responded with silence, until one of the fathers in the group spoke up. He said that he felt fortunate that he was able to bring his family to Riverdale, and he appreciated the teachers, although "this doesn't mean," he added, that "there are no problems for us."

The teacher's defensive, accusatory reaction to the parents shifted the focus of the session from the parents' concerns to the teachers' feelings. This shift put the immigrant parents in the position of having to choose between continuing to present their experiences and concerns or reassuring the teachers that they appreciated their lives in their new community and did not hold the teachers responsible for their difficulties.

This meeting with parents and teachers was the pilot for the second stage of the project. Our plan for the second stage was to translate what we had learned from the first stage into innovative strategies for facilitating dialogue between teachers and immigrant parents. We decided to use the videotapes developed in the first stage of the project again as a cue to stimulate discussion, this time with heterogeneous groups of teachers and parents. This chapter tells the story of our not entirely successful attempt to implement this approach over the course of a year at a single site, Solano Preschool in Phoenix.

THE PROBLEM OF PARENT PARTICIPATION

In designing our strategies for promoting parent-teacher dialogue and cultural negotiation, our aim was to avoid reproducing the asymmetry that has characterized most approaches to bringing parents into the life of the preschool (Lightfoot 2004). A lack of parent involvement too often is posed as a problem in which parents are implicitly blamed for not taking sufficient interest in their children's education. Our research suggests just the opposite. Many parents, including parents who have recently immigrated from another country, have a lot to say about early childhood education and care, a keen interest in what goes on in their children's preschools, and a desire to be more involved in the school.

Parent participation can take many forms (Epstein 1995): coming to school to help out the teachers by preparing curricular materials (for example, cutting out squares and triangles or mixing paint); providing an extra pair of hands on field trips; working on fund-raising projects for the school; and participating in parent-teacher associations (PTAs)—which in the case of preschools are usually MTAs (mother-teacher associations)— which hold meetings at the school every month or so with an agenda more focused on fund-raising than on discussing changes to the curriculum. For immigrant parents, parent participation often takes the form, as in Head Start, of preschool programs expanding their mission from providing education and care to children to also serving parents, with workshops on child development and effective child-raising strategies, English language lessons, social service and mental health referrals, and job training seminars (Lamb et al. 2001). The least common form of parent participation in preschools is any approach in which parents have a significant voice in decisions about curriculum and pedagogy.

Parent involvement always has been a core feature of Head Start, a federal program with a "two-generation" approach to helping children and their families overcome the disadvantages of poverty (Henrick and Gadaire 2008; Marcon 1999). From its inception, there have been struggles within Head Start to define the role of parents (Kuntz 1998; Zigler and

Anderson 1979). These struggles, as Dory Lightfoot (2004, 26) writes, were "between activists who saw poor mothers as deficient and in need of training and those who saw them as powerful and entitled to input in the shaping of the program." These ideological struggles in Head Start echo the tensions of the settlement house era programs of a century earlier (Lissak 1989). We argue that they continue to the present day.

Parent involvement in Head Start includes services *for* parents (parenting and nutrition classes and help in accessing a range of social services) and opportunities for input *by* parents (volunteering in the program and participating in parent committees and policy councils, Castro et al. 2004). The Head Start performance standards state: "Parents must be invited to become integrally involved in the development of the program's curriculum and approach to child development and education" (Office of Head Start 2009, 124). In practice, parental influence is limited by the fact that much of the Head Start curriculum is set at the national level, by accreditation standards, and by the ethos of the program, which at heart views parents from a developmental—if not deficit—perspective as clients in need of services. Parents are encouraged to participate in Head Start policy councils as much to develop a sense of agency and leadership skills and to make them feel less isolated (Small 2009) as to contribute to changes in the program's curriculum or pedagogy. We are not suggesting that many or even most parents with children in Head Start are not in need of support and guidance with child-rearing, referrals to social services, and the chance to gain experience participating in an organization's governance. What we are suggesting is that a program that begins with these goals will always struggle to create a nonhierarchical relationship between staff and parents (Peart and Bryant 2000).

Studies have pointed to the need for better communication between practitioners and parents who do not share a common cultural background or language (Gonzalez et al. 2005; Gonzalez-Mena 2001, 2008; Hayden, De Goia, and Hadley 2003). This is a point emphasized in the report sponsored by the National Research Council on "Cultural Diversity and Early Education" (Phillips and Crowell 1994) and in the Office of Head Start's latest update of "Multicultural Principles for Head Start Programs Serving Children Ages Birth to Five" (2008). Our project builds on this work, but pays more explicit attention to the need not just for more parent education and parent participation, and not just for an open exchange of information between practitioners and parents, but also for a process of "cultural negotiation"—a dialogue that includes discussion about the problems and possibilities of creating preschool programs that reflect the values and beliefs of both the immigrant community and the receiving society (Vandenbroeck et al. 2009).

We should not naively expect that if and when practitioners and parents from different cultural and class backgrounds come together to talk, all will go well. Fabienne Doucet (2008, 2011b) points out that participating in parent involvement activities at their children's school carries the risk of exposing immigrant parents to criticism, condescension, and even being reported to child protective services. Michel Vandenbroeck (2009) suggests that the more parents and practitioners listen to each other, the better they may come to understand the depths of their differences, which in some cases may seem intractable.

What is needed, then, is not just better communication between practitioners and parents but also the willingness and ability on both sides to negotiate across cultural and class divides. We use the word "negotiate" because it carries a sense of politics and power that is not explicitly present in the terms "participation," "dialogue," and "communication." If practitioners and parents engage in negotiation, both have to be prepared to put their beliefs and preferences on the table and to compromise (Hughes and McNaughton 2000; Vandenbroeck 2009). It is critical at the onset of such a project to acknowledge and address the asymmetrical power relationships between school staff and parents, especially when the parents are immigrants. This asymmetry cannot be leveled, but it can be acknowledged and addressed.

It is also critical to recognize that although immigrant parents and their child's preschool teachers share a concern about the well-being of the child they have in common, they also have divergent interests, and therefore, as with workers and management, there will be times when what is best for one side is less good for the other. A simple example from the quotidian routines of preschool life is the question of the length of naptime. Hardworking parents, desperate for a bit of downtime between the time when their child falls asleep at night and when they do, may ask the preschool teacher to not let their child nap very long, so that the child will fall asleep at night at a reasonable hour. Hardworking teachers, desperate for a respite in the middle of their exhausting day, may insist that all children sleep (or at least make no demands on them) for at least an hour of naptime. Such disagreements can be worked out, but only if both sides, parents and teachers, can acknowledge to themselves and each other their personal interests and not pretend that their only concern is the well-being of the child. Compromise is needed, because for one side to gain some power the other side must cede some.

Some of the divergent positions taken by immigrant parents and teachers involve culture. To be a member of a culture is to have strongly felt, taken-for-granted beliefs about such basic questions as what constitutes good parenting and good teaching, how children develop, and whether knowledge is constructed or transmitted, as well as beliefs about food preferences, dietary prohibitions, and gender roles. Preschools are sites where divergent cultural systems come into contact and sometimes clash. Negotiating such fundamental disagreements between new immigrants and their children's preschools is in a sense the essential work of democracy, for what does it mean to be a democracy if not to have citizens work out their disagreements—what Chantal Mouffe (2005) calls their "antagonisms"—about how to organize living together? Participating in a democratic process means that sometimes a consensus emerges, while at other times there is a need for negotiation between parties who hold competing perspectives and interests.

Adding attention to power and self-interest to our thinking about the problem of the participation of immigrant parents in preschools can help us avoid the sentimentality of the more naive approaches to parent participation that make it seem that once we put practitioners and immigrant parents in a room together with coffee and cookies, problems will sort themselves out. Our pilot program in parent-teacher dialogue and negotiation demonstrated to us that bringing parents and teachers together is necessary, but not sufficient. No meaningful success can be achieved without unlearning old patterns; learning to avoid acting out familiar, hierarchical roles; and imagining new ways of talking, relating, and negotiating power.

THE PROGRAM

Our intervention plan was to work for a year with the staff and parents at Solano Preschool, the public preschool in Phoenix where we made the videotape for the first stage of the project. We took our conceptual model from Funds of Knowledge, an approach developed by Norma González, Luis Moll, and Cathy Amanti (2005) for creating curriculum based on the cultural knowledge of the families served by the school.

We began by inviting the seven teachers, the director, and the social worker to join us in a series of weekly meetings where we introduced the Funds of Knowledge approach and brainstormed ideas for involving parents. After a semester of monthly meetings, five of the seven teachers decided not to continue. The other two teachers, Lolie Gomez and Carmen Duron, expressed a willingness to implement the new approach.

In the first gathering with parents, we organized an activity in which parents and teachers met in the school's library to watch and discuss the video we had shot three years earlier in Lolie's class. We provided child care in the classroom, as well as pizza. The activity was successful in terms of the number of parents who attended, but not in producing meaningful dialogue between parents and the teachers. Most of the parents' comments took the form of commending and thanking the teachers for their hard work. One parent hesitantly commented on an activity seen in the video, in which Lolie asks children to draw a picture about a book she has read to them (*Love You Forever*). The parent suggested that perhaps this activity could have been more explicitly structured as an art lesson, with more emphasis on art skills, or on writing. Lolie responded by saying:

> Actually, there was art and writing. It was when they were talking about the mother and the child in the story, who they were drawing. That's why we were writing down words to go with what the children had drawn. That was our small group plan, that teachable moment. That's a teacher-directed activity. The rest of it was constantly, you know, redirecting and teaching them.

Carmen backed Lolie up, emphasizing their philosophy that children learn best through play:

> I know most parents think that when they see children jumping and having a good time that they are not learning. But all the research that has been done. . . . For instance, you see children playing with blocks. They are having a good time stacking them, but they are also learning geometry, learning about shapes. When the child in the video put semicircle blocks together, she said, "That's a doughnut!" and then she said, "That's a circle!" That's a self-discovery kind of experiment that she conducted. Or when they are doing music, they are doing a lot of body awareness. This is where they learn where their body is in space.

Following these explanations from Lolie and Carmen, the mother who had raised the question about giving a more explicitly academic direction to the activity said nothing. When one of us asked her, "Was that what you had in mind, or were you trying to make another point?" she responded, "No, now I see the difference." What we took from this and other similar interactions in this session was that the teachers at this point were unable to hear parents' views on pedagogy and curriculum as anything more than a lack of understanding of their progressive practices, and therefore they felt the need to explain and justify these practices to the parents.

Debriefing these sessions, we collectively decided that in subsequent sessions the teachers might feel less defensive and the parents freer to raise critical points if we used as a cue the videos we made in French and Italian preschools rather than the Solano video. In the next session, we showed the Italian video, but despite our best attempts to moderate and steer the direction of the conversation, it did not produce a real dialogue between parents and the teachers about the curriculum. Interestingly, the most successful conversation was produced by chance in the following session. That evening technical difficulties prevented us from showing the French video we had planned to show, so we instead showed a video we happened to have with us of a day in a Japanese preschool. In this video, there is a scene of a male assistant, in shorts and no shirt, drying off naked children as they change out of their swimming suits. This scene produced a heated response from a Guatemalan parent who said that a man should not be helping children change their clothes. This led to a lively, back-and-forth, symmetrical discussion among the parents and teachers on issues of safety, prevention of sexual abuse, and gender issues. Lolie reported later that this conversation helped her better understand parents' expectations and concerns about bathroom use, privacy, and modesty.

In these initial meetings with teachers and parents, we acted as organizers and sponsors (or as the Mexican parents described our role, as "padrinos"). We helped teachers create flyers, we showed the videos, we moderated the discussions, and we provided food and paid for the child care. Concerned that this approach would not lead to a model of parent involvement that would survive the end of the project, our research team proposed changing the format for the next round of sessions. In an attempt to encourage more dialogue between teachers and parents and give teachers and parents more of a feeling of ownership of the activities, we developed a new strategy in which, instead of meeting in the library and watching and discussing videos, we met in each teacher's classroom, with a theme and activity selected by the teacher and the parents at the previous meeting.

As it turned out, a change we had made in the organization of the food for the evening produced the most significant change in the group dynamics. At the end of the previous meeting, some parents had suggested that instead of our providing pizza, they would bring the food, which would be typical dishes from their homelands. These dishes turned out to be a combination of Mexican stews and Central American pastries.

By this time, we had provided the food, usually pizza, so often that the children had come to call Joe Tobin "Pizza Man." When parents suggested providing the food for the next meeting, we were initially concerned about the costs they would incur. But we came to realize that offering to provide the food was the parents' way of tilting the balance and sharing in the role of being providers and rotating the "padrinazgo." The last meeting of the year took place in Lolie's classroom, where most of the parents were from Mexico. When it was time to eat, the mothers took control, telling the children, husbands, teachers, and research team members to sit down on the small chairs around the low tables. The mothers first served the children, then the men (their husbands and Joe Tobin), and then Angela Arzubiaga and Jennifer Adair, then the women teachers, and finally themselves. While hardly a sign of progress on the gender equity front, serving their husbands before the teachers and the women research team members could be seen as an act of cultural empowerment. On the one hand, we were concerned that our parent-teacher dialogue plans had evolved into a Mexican social event. But on the other hand, we were encouraged that the meetings were evolving and we could see the beginnings of a transformation. By not only preparing the meal, which was all traditional dishes from their homelands, but also serving it following their cultural customs of having men eat before women, these parents transformed the setting from one where parents adapted to the routines of the school to a Mexican–Central American cultural space.

With the transformation of the food and meeting style, parents gained more confidence. For example, in an after-dinner discussion about immigration, a mother teasingly referred to Lolie, who herself came to the United States from Mexico as a teenager, as "La Coyota," a joke making use of the feminine form for the people who illegally bring immigrants over the border, for a fee, into the United States. We saw in this change in tone a sign of the development of trust and the equalizing of power. Such a shift is necessary to create the conditions for symmetrical dialogue between teachers and immigrant parents.

As the year drew to a close, we asked parents for concrete suggestions on what could be done to create ongoing structures for more active parent participation and voice in the school. Having come to know each other over the course of the year, and having developed an appreciation for what could be gained with more parent involvement, this group of parents generated some useful suggestions. They emphasized that meetings held during the day precluded attendance by working parents, and that meetings held on week nights were difficult because parents were tired and stressed. Their solution was to schedule some weekend activities for families to come together to socialize and exchange ideas with each other and with teachers and the director.

Another suggestion was to move the site of parent-teacher gathering from the school to a neighborhood park, where the mood could be more relaxed and children could play while their parents and teachers talked. We heard in this suggestion the implication that many parents felt uncomfortable at school. As a father jokingly said: "When I am here at school, I always feel like I am about to be sent to the principal's office."

The mothers suggested creating a place for parents to meet at school.

Mothers said that they appreciated the moments they had to talk to each other and to the teachers when they dropped off and picked up their children, but that these encounters were awkward because everyone was standing up and caught up in the tasks of saying good-bye to their children, signing in, and so forth. Something as simple as setting up a table next door to the classroom and providing coffee, they suggested, could lead to more parent involvement.

As this meeting, the last of the year, was coming to an end, we asked the parents and teachers if they would like to continue the gatherings the following year. Most of the parents pointed out that, while they had enjoyed and benefited from the meetings, they would not have children in the preschool the next school year. This led to the suggestion to begin the following school year with a meeting for the new group of parents to select a representative or a small team to organize and facilitate meetings and social activities and to bring concerns back and forth between the teachers and parents. One parent suggested that this could perhaps be made a paid position. A few of the parents expressed a willingness to attend a parent-teacher meeting in the fall to give new parents the benefit of their perspectives and experience.

WHAT WAS ACCOMPLISHED?

While we were working with Solano Preschool, a group of immigrant parents became more active and empowered and changed the nature of the parent-teacher meetings, but as mentioned, because most members of this group did not have children in the preschool the following year, the process needed to be restarted again the next fall with a new group of parents. Once our research team ceased to play a role in facilitating them, the formal parent-teacher dialogue meetings ended.

Our intervention effort suggests that multiple factors make it difficult for immigrant parents to speak and be heard at their children's preschools:

- Unfamiliarity with the task of engaging in discussion with teachers. All forms of conversation are conventional, and those not familiar with the conventions find engagement in the conversation difficult.

- Discomfort being in school (for some parents, because of bad memories from their own student days).

- Scheduling difficulties, especially those arising from conflicts with work.

- Language barriers, which produce in immigrant parents not just an inability to express themselves but also frustration that the version of themselves they are expressing when speaking a second language may come across as unsophisticated, banal, or ignorant.

- A tendency (stronger among some immigrant communities than others) to show deference to teachers and to the host society, even when not in agreement. Teachers often mistake immigrant parents' deference for agreement.

- A fearfulness among immigrant parents that complaining or even making suggestions may provoke negative reactions from school staff directed at them or their children. This can lead to the related fear that speaking out can be a trap and that it is safer to say nothing (Doucet 2008, 2011b).

- Fatalism ("Nothing I can say to teachers will make a difference, so why try?").

- Parents' social isolation and economic stress, which may make it difficult for them to attend meetings and to form alliances with other immigrant parents when they do (Lamb-Parker et al. 2001).

Most immigrant parents do not come to school as members of an established, preexisting group. They often come to school not knowing the other parents with children in the same class on more than a nodding basis. They often live in communities that provide few opportunities to find common cause with other immigrants or to get to know non-immigrants. Some immigrant parents transcend these barriers and speak up in meetings at school, but they do not necessarily represent those who do not speak; the most alienated, recently arrived, and deferential of immigrant parents are the least likely to come to meetings at their children's preschools or to speak when they do.

CREATING CONTEXTS FOR DIALOGUE BETWEEN IMMIGRANT PARENTS AND TEACHERS

Any top-down directive to teachers to engage with parents is likely to be met with resistance. The first task of an effort to create dialogue between teachers and immigrant parents is therefore to address and acknowledge teachers' concerns. The impetus for giving immigrant parents' greater voice is unlikely to come from the teachers in a preschool. But because teachers' sincere and enthusiastic participation in creating a new approach is needed, it is critical at the start to enlist their support and to recognize that this process will take time and cannot be achieved overnight.

The concept of entering into dialogue with teachers about the curriculum is no more familiar to parents than it is to teachers. Groundwork therefore also needs to be done with parents. Before immigrant parents can speak up and be heard in a meaningful way in preschools, they first need to get to know each other, to recognize their common interests, and to become a community rather than a collection of individual voices. Most preschool parents do not know each other well, rarely interact, and do not realize that they have common concerns. Parents in general and immigrant parents in particular hesitate for many reasons to speak up in discussions with teachers, including fear of exacerbating their marginality by making explicit their areas of disagreement with the beliefs and practices of the host society and a fear of offending their children's teachers and thereby provoking retaliation. Because these fears are not entirely without basis, immigrant parents should be counseled to be strategic and even guarded in their dialogue with teachers, at least initially.

Learning to talk with teachers is a process that takes time. The challenge is especially daunting because parents are not long-term members of a preschool community. In many locations, parents have their children in a preschool class only for one year, which is just barely enough time for parents to get to know each other and to start getting organized and comfortable entering into dialogue with teachers. Each year in a preschool class the process needs to be started anew. Mario Small (2009) suggests that participating in the life of their children's preschool program can be an important source of informal networking and social connection for poor mothers. Our sense is that many of the immigrant mothers appreciate the chance to meet and talk with other mothers when they drop off and pick up their children at the beginning and end of the school day, but that the organized parent activities rarely produce a sense of camaraderie or connection among parents. The fact that most parents are members of a preschool community for only one or two years also works against the preschool becoming a pivotal networking point in their lives.

For a program of parent-teacher dialogue to be implemented successfully in a preschool, there must be not just a desire for this from parents and a willingness from teachers but also structural support. Preschool teachers and directors, already feeling burdened by the expectations placed on them, tend to resist investing scarce time and energy in the implementation of programs for additional dialogue with parents. And there are, of course, problems with top-down directives: they may not be welcomed by those below; they may be implemented cynically; and they may disappear when the mandate shifts and the money that incentivized their implementation runs out. But despite these concerns, as well as our preference for ground-up, grassroots initiatives, our conclusion is that without such pressures, direction, and financial incentives from above, the kind of paradigm shift required to give immigrant parents voice in preschools is unlikely to happen.

Because it is unrealistic to expect immigrant parents and their children's teachers to establish mechanisms for parent-teacher dialogue on their own, it is crucial that preschool directors play a central role. Preschools with effective communication between parents and staff often employ the services of a parent-teacher liaison or family support worker. Large preschool programs, including those located within public schools, often have funds for such a position. In smaller programs that are not as well funded, a socially skilled bilingual and bicultural member of the office staff sometimes plays the role of parent-teacher liaison.

When immigrant parents come together with non-immigrant parents and with teachers, we should have modest expectations. Arguments, tensions, and frustrations on all sides are to be expected. In fact, an absence of disagreement and tension can be taken as a sign that the participants are not yet really engaging with each other. As Michel Vandenbroeck argues in his 2009 essay "Let Us Disagree," diversity of cultures in a preschool, like cultural diversity in the larger society, requires an acceptance of the inevitability of disagreements and therefore the creation of structures where these disagreements can be debated.

We should not naively believe that introducing parent-teacher dialogue and ways to negotiate the curriculum will make things better in a preschool for teachers, parents, or children. It must be acknowledged from the start that such a process carries risks as well as the potential for gains. Once real dialogue begins, things are likely to get worse for a while before they get better as teachers and parents, immigrants and non-immigrants, discover that some of their differences are not easily reconciled (Vandenbroeck et al. 2009). As Christa Preissing (2007) eloquently states, "What if we really listened to the immigrant parents' voices and they have desires, requests, convictions that are counter to ours? Then what do we do?"

Models of parent-teacher dialogue must be appropriate for the specific local context. Rather than attempting to identify a single best practice for promoting dialogue between practitioners and immigrant parents, we conclude that the best approach is one that supports preschools by giving them the latitude and resources to create their own models that are appropriate for their local conditions and responsive to their local community.

References

Adair, Jennifer. 2011. "Confirming *Chanclas:* What Early Childhood Teacher Educators Can Learn from Immigrant Preschool Teachers and Their Critique of Language 'Modeling' Techniques." *Journal of Early Childhood Teacher Education* 32(1): 55–71.

———. 2012. "Discrimination as a Contextualized Obstacle to Teaching Young Latino Children of Immigrants." *Contemporary Issues in Early Childhood Education* 13(3): 163–74.

———. Forthcoming. "Examining Whiteness as an Obstacle to Positively Approaching Immigrant Families in United States Early Childhood Educational Settings." *Race, Ethnicity, and Education.*

Adair, Jennifer, and Giulia Pastori. 2011. "Developing Qualitative Coding Frameworks for Educational Research: Immigration, Education, and the Children Crossing Borders Project." *International Journal of Research and Method in Education* 34(1): 31–47.

Adair, Jennifer Keys, Joseph Tobin, and Angela E. Arzubiaga. 2012. "The Dilemma of Cultural Responsiveness and Professionalization: Listening Closer to Immigrant Teachers Who Teach Children of Recent Immigrants." *Teachers College Record* 114(12): 1–37.

Akhtar, Salman.1999. "The Immigrant, the Exile, and the Experience of Nostalgia." *Journal of Applied Psychoanalytic Studies* 1(2): 123–30.

Anzaldúa, Gloria. 1999. *Borderlands: La Frontera.* San Francisco: Aunt Lute.

Arzubiaga, Angela E., and Jennifer Adair. 2009. "Misrepresentations of Language and Culture, Language and Culture as Proxies for Marginalization: Debunking the Arguments." In *Handbook of Latinos and Education,* edited by Enrique Murillo. Mahwah, N.J.: Lawrence Erlbaum Associates.

Arzubiaga, Angela, Sylvia Noguerón, and Amanda Sullivan. 2009. "The Education of Children in Im/migrant Families." *Review of Research in Education* 33(1): 246–71.

Bakhtin, Mikhail. 1990. *Art and Answerability.* Translated by Michael Holquist and Vadim Liapunov. Austin: University of Texas Press.

Balibar, Etienne. 2003. *We, the People of Europe? Reflections on Transnational Citizenship*. Princeton, N.J.: Princeton University Press.

Ballenger, Cynthia. 1998. *Teaching Other People's Children: Literacy and Learning in a Bilingual Classroom*. New York: Teachers College Press.

Bartlett, Kathy. 2012. "The Integrated Madrasa Preschool Project." In *Learning and Teaching About Islam: Essays in Understanding*, edited by Caroline Ellwood. Melton, U.K.: John Catt Educational.

Beatty, Barbara. 1997. *Preschool Education in America: The Culture of Young Children from the Colonial Era to the Present*. New Haven, Conn.: Yale University Press.

Beller, Simone. 2008. "Fostering Language Acquisition in Daycare Settings: What Does the Research Tell Us?" Working Paper 49. The Hague: Bernard van Leer Foundation.

Berg, Ellen. 2010. "Linked with the Welfare of All Peoples': The American Kindergarten, Americanization, and Internationalism in World War I." In *Raising Citizens in the "Century of the Child": Child Rearing in America and Europe, 1900–2000*, edited by Dirk Schumann. Oxford: Berghahn Books.

Bodrova, Elena. 2008. "Make-Believe Play Versus Academic Skills: A Vygotskian Approach to Today's Dilemma of Early Childhood Education." *European Early Childhood Education Research Journal* 16(3): 357–69.

Brougère, Gilles, Nacira Guénif-Souilamas, and Sylvie Rayna. 2008. "*École Maternelle* [Preschool] in France: A Cross-Cultural Perspective." *European Early Childhood Education Research Journal* 16(3): 371–84.

Brown, Christopher. 2009. "Pivoting a Prekindergarten Program Off the Child or the Standard? A Case Study of Integrating the Practices of Early Childhood Education into Elementary School." *Elementary School Journal* 110(2): 202–27.

Capps, Randolph, Michael E. Fix, Julie Murray, Jason Ost, Jeffrey S. Passel, and Shinta Hernandez. 2005. *The New Demography of America's Schools: Immigration and the No Child Left Behind Act*. Washington, D.C.: Urban Institute.

Carlson, Stephanie, and Andrew Meltzoff. 2008. "Bilingual Experience and Executive Functioning in Young Children." *Developmental Science* 11(2): 282–98.

Carreón, Gustavo Pérez, Corey Drake, and Angela Barton. 2005. "The Importance of Presence: Immigrant Parents' School Engagement Experiences." *American Educational Research Journal* 42(3): 465–98.

Castro, Dina, Donna Bryant, Ellen Peisner-Feinberg, and Martie Skinner. 2004. "Parent Involvement in Head Start Programs: The Role of Parent, Teacher, and Classroom Characteristics." *Early Childhood Research Quarterly* 19(3): 413–30.

Chrispeels, Janet, and Elvia Rivero. 2001. "Engaging Latino Families for Student Success: How Parent Education Can Reshape Parents' Sense of Place in the Education of Their Children." *Peabody Journal of Education* 76(2): 119–69.

Copple, Carol, and Sue Bradekamp. 2011. *Developmentally Appropriate Practice in Early Childhood Programs Serving Children from Birth Through Age Eight*. Washington, D.C.: National Association for the Education of Young Children.

Cornfield, Daniel B., and Angela Arzubiaga. 2004. "Immigrants and Education in the U.S. Interior: Integrating and Segmenting Tendencies in Nashville, Tennessee." *Peabody Journal of Education* 79(2): 157–79.

Crosnoe, Robert. 2007. "Early Child Care and the School Readiness of Children from Mexican Immigrant Families." *International Migration Review* 41(1): 152–81.

Daniel, Jerlean, and Susan Friedman. 2005. "Preparing Teachers to Work with Culturally and Linguistically Diverse Children." *Young Children* 60(6): 1–7.

Darling-Hammond, Linda. 2007. "Race, Inequality, and Educational Accountability: The Irony of 'No Child Left Behind.'" *Race, Ethnicity, and Education* 10(3): 245–60.

De Gaetano, Yvonne. 2007. "The Role of Culture in Engaging Latino Parents' Involvement in School." *Urban Education* 42(2): 145–62.

De Gaetano, Yvonne, Leslie R. Williams, and Dinah Volk. 1998. *Kaleidoscope: A Multicultural Approach for the Primary School Classroom*. Upper Saddle River, N.J.: Merrill.

Delgado-Gaitan, Concha, and Henry Trueba. 1991. *Crossing Cultural Borders: Education for Immigrant Families in America*. New York: Routledge.

Delpit, Lisa. 1995. *Other People's Children: Cultural Conflict in the Classroom*. New York: New Press.

Doucet, Fabienne. 2008. "How African American Parents Understand Their and Teachers' Roles in Children's Schooling and What This Means for Preparing Preservice Teachers." *Journal of Early Childhood Teacher Education* (special issue on "Multicultural Teacher Education in Honor of Leslie R. Williams") 29(2): 108–39.

———. 2011a. "Parent Involvement as Ritualized Practice." *Anthropology and Education Quarterly* 42(4): 404–21.

———. 2011b. "(Re)Constructing Home and School: Immigrant Parents, Agency, and the (Un)Desirability of Bridging Multiple Worlds." *Teachers College Record* 113(12): 2705–38.

Dyson, Anne. 2003. "Popular Literacies and the 'All' Children: Rethinking Literacy Development for Contemporary Childhoods." *Language Arts* 81(2): 100–9.

Early, Diane M., Donna M. Bryant, Robert C. Pianta, Richard M. Clifford, Margaret R. Burchinal, Sharon Ritchie, Carollee Howes, and Oscar Barbarin. 2006. "Are Teachers' Education, Major, and Credentials Related to Classroom Quality and Children's Academic Gains in Prekindergarten?" *Early Childhood Research Quarterly* 21(2): 174–95.

Early, Diane, Kelly L. Maxwell, Margaret Burchinal, et al. 2007. "Teachers' Education, Classroom Quality, and Young Children's Academic Skills: Results from Seven Studies of Preschool Programs." *Child Development* 78(2): 558–80.

Early, Diane, and Pamela Winton. 2001. "Preparing the Workforce: Early Childhood Teacher Preparation at Two- and Four-Year Institutions of Higher Education." *Early Childhood Research Quarterly* 16(3): 285–306.

Epstein, Joyce. 1995. "School/Family/Community Partnerships: Caring for the Children We Share." *Phi Delta Kappan* 76(9): 701–12.

Evans, Bruce, and Nancy Hornberger. 2005. "No Child Left Behind: Repealing and Unpeeling Federal Language Education Policy in the United States." *Language Policy* 4(1): 87–106.

Fass, Paula. 2006. *Children of a New World: Society, Culture, and Globalization.* New York: New York University Press.

Fillmore, Lily Wong. 1991. "When Learning a Second Language Means Losing the First." *Early Childhood Research Quarterly* 6(3): 323–46.

Fisher, Patrick. 2012. "'The God Gap' and the Political Consequences of Secularization." Paper presented at the Annual Meeting of the Western Political Science Association, Portland, Oregon, March 22–24, 2012.

Foner, Nancy. 2005. "Then and Now or Then to Now: Immigration to New York in Contemporary and Historical Perspective." *Journal of American Ethnic History* 25(2/3): 33–47.

Fortuny, Karina, Donald J. Hernandez, and Ajay Chaudry. 2010. *Young Children of Immigrants: The Leading Edge of America's Future.* Washington, D.C.: Urban Institute.

Freire, Paolo. 1970. *Pedagogy of the Oppressed.* New York: Continuum.

———. 1974. *Education for Critical Consciousness.* New York: Continuum Impacts.

Fuller, Bruce. 2007. *Standardized Childhoods: The Political and Cultural Struggle over Early Education.* Stanford, Calif.: Stanford University Press.

Fusarelli, Lance. 2004. "The Potential Impact of the No Child Left Behind Act on Equity and Diversity in American Education." *Educational Policy* 18(1): 71–94.

Garcia, Eugene. 2005. *Teaching and Learning in Two Languages: Bilingualism and Schooling in the United States.* New York: Teachers College Press.

———. 2007. *Para nuestros niños: Expanding and Improving Early Education for Hispanics: Executive Report.* National Taskforce on Early Childhood Education for Hispanics, Tempe, AZ (March).

Garcia, Eugene, Ann-Marie Wiese, and Delis Cuéller. 2011. "Language, Public Policy, and Schooling: A Focus on Chicano English Language Learners." In *Chicano School Failure and Success: Past, Present, and Future,* 3rd ed., edited by Richard Valencia. New York: Routledge.

Genishi, Celia, and A. Lin Goodwin. 2008. *Diversities in Early Childhood Education: Rethinking and Doing.* New York: Routledge.

Gogolin, Ingrid. 2002. "Linguistic and Cultural Diversity In Europe: A Challenge for Educational Research and Practice." *European Educational Research Journal* 1(1): 123–38.

Goldenberg, Claude, and Ronald Gallimore. 1995. "Immigrant Latino Parents' Values and Beliefs About Their Children's Education: Continuities and Discontinuities Across Cultures and Generations." In *Advances in Motivation and Achievement,* vol. 9, edited by Martin L. Maehr and Paul R. Pinrich. Bingley, U.K.: Emerald Group Publishing Limited.

Goldenberg, Claude, Ronald Gallimore, Leslie Reese, and Helen Garnier. 2001. "Cause or Effect? A Longitudinal Study of Immigrant Latino Parents' Aspirations and Expectations and Their Children's School Performance." *American Educational Research Association Journal* 38(3): 547–82.

González, Norma, Luis Moll, and Cathy Amanti. 2005. *Funds of Knowledge: Theorizing Practices in Households, Communities, and Classrooms.* Hillsdale, N.J.: Lawrence Erlbaum Associates.

Gonzalez-Mena, Janet. 2001. *Foundations: Early Childhood Education in a Diverse Society.* Mountain View, Calif.: Mayfield.

———. 2008. *Diversity in Early Care and Education: Honoring Differences,* 5th ed. Washington, D.C.: National Association for the Education of Young Children.

Goodwin, A. Lin. 2002. "Teacher Preparation and the Education of Immigrant Children." *Education and Urban Society* 34(2): 156–72.

Graue, Mary Elizabeth. 2005. "Theorizing and Describing Preservice Teachers' Images of Families and Schooling." *Teachers College Record* 107(1): 157–85.

Guénif-Souilamas, Nacira. 2006. *La République mise à nu par son immigration.* Paris: La Fabrique Editions.

Harwood, Robin, Birgit Leyendecker, Vivian Carlson, Marysol Asencio, and Amy Miller. 2002. "Parenting Among Latino Families in the U.S." In *Handbook of Parenting,* vol. 4, *Social Conditions and Applied Parenting,* edited by M. H. Bornstein. Mahwah, N.J.: Lawrence Erlbaum Associates.

Hayden, Jacqueline, Katey De Goia, and Fay Hadley. 2003. "Enhancing Partnerships and Networks with Culturally and Linguistically Diverse Families in Early Childhood Settings." Sydney, Australia: University of Western Sydney and New South Wales Department of Community Services.

Henrich, Christopher, and Dana Gadaire. 2008. "Head Start and Parent Involvement." *Infants and Young Children* 21(1): 56–69.

Henry, Hani, William Stiles, and Mia Biran. 2005. "Loss and Mourning in Immigration: Using the Assimilation Model to Assess Continuing Bonds with Native Culture." *Counseling Psychology Quarterly* 18(2): 109–19.

Horne, Thomas, Superintendent of Public Instruction, Arizona State Department of Education. 2007. "An Open Letter to the Citizens of Tucson" (June 11). Available at: http://nau.edu/uploadedFiles/Academic/CAL/Philosophy/Forms/An%20Open%20Letter%20to%20Citizens%20of%20Tucson.pdf (accessed October 2, 2011).

Hughes, Patrick, and Glenda McNaughton. 2000. "Consensus, Dissensus, or Community: The Politics of Parent Involvement in Early Childhood Education." *Contemporary Issues in Early Childhood* 1(3): 241–58.

Kagan, Sharon, and Kristie Kauerz. 2006. "Making the Most of Kindergarten: Trends and Policy Issues." In *Teaching and Learning in the Kindergarten Year,* edited by D. Gullo. Washington, D.C.: National Association for the Education of Young Children.

Katz, Lilian. 1999. "Curriculum Disputes in Early Childhood Education." *ERIC Digest* EDO-PS-99-13 (December).

Kouritzin, G. Sandra. 1999. *Face[t]s of First Language Loss*. Mahwah, N.J.: Lawrence Erlbaum Associates.

Kuntz, Katherine. 1998. "A Lost Legacy: Head Start's Origins in Community Action." In *Critical Perspectives on Project Head Start: Revisioning the Hope and Challenge*, edited by Jeanne Ellsworth and Lynda Ames. Albany, NY: SUNY Press.

Kymlicka, Will. 2001. *Politics in the Vernacular: Nationalism, Multiculturalism, and Citizenship*. Oxford: Oxford University Press.

Lamb-Parker, Faith, Chaya Piotrkowksi, Amy Baker, Susan Kessler-Sklar, Beryl Clark, and Lenore Peay. 2001. "Understanding Barriers to Parent Involvement in Head Start: A Research-Community Partnership." *Early Childhood Research Quarterly* 16(1): 35–51.

Lareau, Annette. 2003. *Unequal Childhoods: Class, Race, and Family Life*. Berkeley: University of California Press.

Lee, Jongho, and Harry Pachon. 2007. "Leading the Way: An Analysis of the Effect of Religion on the Latino Vote." *American Politics Research* 35(2): 252–72.

LeVine, Robert, and Merry White. 1986. *Human Conditions: The Cultural Basis of Educational Development*. Boston: Routledge & Kegan Paul.

Lightfoot, Dory. 2004. "'Some Parents Just Don't Care': Decoding the Meanings of Parental Involvement in Urban Schools." *Urban Education* 39(1): 91–107.

Lijtmaer, Ruth. 2001. "Splitting and Nostalgia in Recent Immigrants: Psychodynamic Considerations." *Journal of the American Academy of Psychoanalysis* 29(3): 427–38.

Lim, Chi-Ing, Kelly Maxwell, Harriet Able-Boone, and Catherine Zimmer. 2009. "Cultural and Linguistic Diversity in Early Childhood Teacher Preparation: The Impact of Contextual Characteristics on Coursework and Practica." *Early Childhood Research Quarterly* 24(1): 64–76.

Lindholm-Leary, Kathryn, and Graciela Borsato. 2006. "Academic Achievement." In *Educating English Language Learners: A Synthesis of Research Evidence*, edited by Fred Genesee, Kathryn Lindholm-Leary, William Saunders, and Donna Christian. New York: Cambridge University Press.

Lissak, Rivka.1983. "A Benefit-Cost Analysis of the Abecedarian Early Childhood Intervention." *Journal of American Ethnic History* 2(2): 21–50.

———. 1989. *Pluralism and Progressives: Hull House and the New Immigrants, 1890–1919*. Chicago: University of Chicago Press.

Loeb, Susanna, Bruce Fuller, Sharon Lynn Kagan, and Bidemi Carrol. 2004. "Child Care in Poor Communities: Early Learning Effects of Type, Quality, and Stability." *Child Development* 75(1): 47–65.

Lonigan, Christopher, and Beth Phillips. 2012. "Understanding the Contributions of Early Academic Skills to Children's Success in School." In *Contemporary De-*

bates in Childhood Education and Development, edited by Sebastian Suggat and Elaine Reese. Abingdon, Canada: Routledge.

López, Gerardo. 2009. "The Value of Hard Work: Lessons on Parent Involvement from an (Im)migrant Household." *Harvard Education Review* 71(3): 416–38.

Louie, Vivian. 2004. *Compelled to Excel: Immigration, Education, and Opportunity among Chinese Americans.* Palo Alto, Calif.: Stanford University Press.

Lucero, Audrey. 2010. "Dora's Program: A Constructively Marginalized Paraeducator and Her Developmental Biliteracy Program." *Anthropology and Education Quarterly* 41(2): 126–43.

MacSwan, Jeffrey, and Lisa Pray. 2005. "Learning English Bilingually: Age of Onset of Exposure and Rate of Acquisition Among English Language Learners in a Bilingual Education Program." *Bilingual Research Journal* 29(3): 653–78.

Mahalingam, Ramaswami. 2006. "Cultural Psychology of Immigrants: An Introduction." In *Cultural Psychology of Immigrants*, edited by Ramaswami Mahalingam. Mahwah, N.J.: Lawrence Erlbaum Associates.

Marcon, Rebecca. 1999. "Differential Impact of Preschool Models on Development and Early Learning of Inner-City Children: A Three Cohort Study." *Developmental Psychology* 35(2): 358–75.

———. 2012. "The Importance of Balance in Early Childhood." In *Contemporary Debates in Childhood Education and Development*, edited by Sebastian Suggat and Elaine Reese. Abingdon, Ontario, Canada: Routledge.

Masse, Leonard, and W. Steven Barnett. 2002. "A Benefit-Cost Analysis of the Abecedarian Early Childhood Intervention." New Brunswick, N.J.: National Institute for Early Education Research (NIEER). Available at: http://nieer.org/resources/research/AbecedarianStudy.pdf (accessed September 1, 2011).

Matute-Bianchi, Maria. 2008. "Situational Ethnicity and Patterns of School Performance among Immigrant and Nonimmigrant Mexican-Descent Students." In *Minority Status, Oppositional Culture, and Schooling*, edited by John Ogbu. New York: Routledge.

Mayo, Yoldana. 1997. "Machismo, Fatherhood, and the Latino Family: Understanding the Concept." *Journal of Multicultural Social Work* 5(1–2): 46–61.

McCartney, Kathleen. 2004. "Current Research on Child Care Effects." *Encyclopedia of Early Childhood Development*. Available at: http://www.enfant-encyclopedie.com/pages/pdf/mccartneyangxp.pdf (accessed July 20, 2012).

Mirande, Alfredo. 1991. "Ethnicity and Fatherhood." In *Fatherhood and Families in Cultural Context*, edited by Frederick W. Bozett and Shirley M. H. Hanson. New York: Springer.

Mitakidou, Soula, Evangelia Tressou, Beth Blue Swadener, and Carl A. Grant, eds. 2009. *Beyond Pedagogies of Exclusion in Diverse Childhood Contexts.* New York: Palgrave Macmillan.

Montejano, David. 1999. *Chicano Politics and Society in the Late Twentieth Century.* Austin: University of Texas Press.

Monzó, Lilla, and Robert Rueda. 2008. "Shaping Education Through Diverse Funds of Knowledge: A Look at One Latina Paraeducator's Lived Experiences, Beliefs, and Teaching Practice." *Anthropology and Education Quarterly* 34(1): 72–95.

Moraga, Cherríe. 1994. "From a Long Line of Vendidas: Chicanas and Feminism." In *Theorizing Feminism: Parallel Trends in the Humanities and Social Sciences*, edited by Anne C. Herrmann and Abigail J. Stewart. Boulder: Westview.

Morton, Rebecca. 2011. "The Non-Cognitive Challenge to a Liberal Egalitarian Education." *Theory and Research in Education* 9(3): 233–50.

Mouffe, Chantal, ed. 2005. *On the Political*. London: Routledge.

Murillo, Enrique. 2002. "How Does It Feel to Be a Problem? 'Disciplining' the Transnational Subject in the American South." In *Education in the New Latino Diaspora*, edited by Stanton Wortham, Enrique G. Murillo Jr., and Edmund T. Hamann. Westport, Conn.: Greenwood Publishing.

Myers, Robert. 2005. "In Search of Quality in Programs of Early Childhood Care and Education (ECCE)." Paper prepared for *EFA Global Monitoring Report 2005: Education for All: The Quality Imperative*. Paris: UNESCO.

National Association for the Education of Young Children (NAEYC). 2009a. "Position Statement on School Readiness." Available at: http://www.naeyc.org/positionstatements/school_readiness (accessed October 1, 2012).

———. 2009b. "Position Statement on Learning to Read and Write." Available at: http://www.naeyc.org/positionstatements (accessed October 1, 2012).

National Institute for Early Education Research (NIEER). 2011. *The State of Preschool 2011*. Rutgers, N.J.: NIEER.

Nores, Milagros, Clive R. Belfeld, W. Steven Barnett, Lawrence Schweinhart, et al. 2005. "Updating the Economic Impacts of the High/Scope Perry Preschool Program." *Educational Evaluation and Policy Analysis* 27(3): 245–61.

Office of Head Start. 2008. *Revisiting and Updating the Multicultural Principles for Head Start Programs Serving Children Ages Birth to Five: Addressing Culture and Home Language in Head Start Program Systems and Services*. Washington: U.S. Department of Health and Human Services, Administration for Children and Families, Office of Head Start.

———. 2009. *Head Start Program Performance Standards*. 45 CFR Chapter XIII (10-1-09 Edition). Washington: U.S. Department of Health and Human Services, Administration for Children and Families, Office of Head Start.

Parke, Ross, and Raymond Buriel. 1998. "Socialization in the Family: Ethnic and Ecological Perspectives." In *Handbook of Child Psychology*, 5th ed., vol. 3, edited by Nancy Eisenberg. New York: John Wiley & Sons.

Peart, Norman, and Donna Bryant. 2000. "Bringing Reality to the Table: Contributors to the Lack of Parent Participation in an Early Childhood Service Program." *Administration in Social Work* 24(4): 21–37.

Pease-Alvarez, Lucinda. 2002. "Moving Beyond Linear Trajectories of Language

Shift and Bilingual Language Socialization." *Hispanic Journal of Behavioral Sciences* 24(2): 114–37.

Phillips, Deborah, and Nancy A. Crowell, eds. 1994. Report of a Workshop. Board on Children and Families, Commission on Behavioral and Social Sciences and Education, National Research Council, 2101 Constitution Avenue, N.W., Washington, D.C. 20418.

Pianta, Robert C., Steven Barnett, Margaret Burchinal, and Kathy Thornburg. 2009. "The Effects of Preschool Education: What We Know, How Public Policy Is or Is Not Aligned with the Evidence Base, and What We Need to Know." *Psychological Science in the Public Interest* 10(2): 49–88.

Portes, Alejandro, Patricia Fernandez-Kelly, and William Haller. 2005. "Segmented Assimilation on the Ground: The New Second Generation in Early Adulthood." *Ethnic and Racial Studies* 28(6): 1000–40.

Portes, Alejandro, and Min Zhou. 1993. "The New Second Generation: Segmented Assimilation and Its Variants Among Post-1965 Immigrant Youth." *Annals of the American Academy of Political and Social Science* 530(1): 74–98.

Preissing, Christa. 2007. "How Can Parents Have a Say in the Follow-up of Quality in Early Childhood Education and Care?" (lecture). Leuven, Belgium: OECD–Starting Strong Network (November).

Qin, Desiree Baolian. 2006. "'Our Child Doesn't Talk to Us Anymore': Alienation in Immigrant Chinese Families." *Anthropology and Education Quarterly* 37(2): 162–79.

Race to the Top. 2011. "Race to the Top—Early Learning Challenge (RTT-ELC) Program Comments." Washington: U.S. Department of Education. Available at: http://www.ed.gov/early-learning/elc-draft-summary (accessed February 7, 2012).

Ramirez, Fred. 2003. "Dismay and Disappointment: Parental Involvement of Latino Immigrant Parents." *Urban Review* 35(2): 93–110.

Ray, Aisha, Barbara Bowman, and Jean Robbins. 2006. "Preparing Early Childhood Teachers to Successfully Educate All Children: The Contribution of Four-Year Undergraduate Teacher Preparation Programs." Report to the Foundation for Child Development. April. Available at: http://www.erikson.edu/wp-content/uploads/Teachered.pdf (accessed April 10, 2012).

Reese, Leslie, Silvia Balzano, Ronald Gallimore, and Claude Goldenberg. 1995. "The Concept of Educación: Latino Family Values and American Schooling." *International Journal of Educational Research* 23(1): 57–81.

Reese, Leslie, and Ronald Gallimore. 2000. "Immigrant Latinos' Cultural Model of Literacy Development: An Evolving Perspective on Home-School Discontinuities." *American Journal of Education* 108(2): 103–34.

Reynolds, Arthur J. 2003. "Age 21 Cost-Benefit Analysis of the Title I Chicago Child/Parent Centers." *Education Evaluation and Policy Analysis* 24(4): 267–303.

Riojas-Cortez, Mari. 2001. "Preschoolers' Funds of Knowledge Displayed Through

Sociodramatic Play Episodes in a Bilingual Classroom." *Early Childhood Education Journal* 29(1): 35–40.

Ritchie, Jenny, and Cheryl Rau. 2008. "Te Puawaitanga: Partnerships with Tamariki and Whānau in Bicultural Early Childhood Care and Education." Wellington, New Zealand: Teaching and Learning Initiative.

Rogoff, Barbara. 2003. *The Cultural Nature of Human Development.* New York: Oxford University Press.

Rueda, Robert, and Lili Monzó. 2002. "Apprenticeship for Teaching: Professional Development Issues Surrounding the Collaborative Relationship Between Teachers and Paraeducators." *Teaching and Teacher Education* 18(5): 503–21.

Rueda, Robert, Lilia Monzó, and Ignacio Higareda. 2004. "Appropriating the Sociocultural Resources of Latino Paraeducators for Effective Instruction with Latino Students: Promise and Problems." *Urban Education* 39(1): 52–90.

Santa Ana, Otto. 2002. *Brown Tide Rising: Metaphors of Latinos in Contemporary American Public Discourse.* Austin: University of Texas Press.

Schildkraut, Debora J. 2005. *Press "One" for English: Language Policy, Public Opinion, and American Identity.* Princeton, N.J.: Princeton University Press.

Schweinhart, Lawrence, Helen Barnes, and David Weikart. 1993. *Significant Benefits: High/Scope Perry Pre-School Study Through Age 27.* Ypsilanti, Mich.: High Scope Press.

Small, Mario. 2009. *Unanticipated Gain: Origins of Network Inequality in Everyday Life.* New York: Oxford University Press.

Smith, Robert. 2005. *Mexican New York: Transnational Lives of New Immigrants.* Berkeley: University of California Press.

Soltero-González, Lucinda. 2008. "The Hybrid Literacy Practices of Young Immigrant Children: Lessons Learned from an English-Only Preschool Classroom." *Bilingual Research Journal* 31(1–2): 75–93.

Soto, Lourdes Diaz. 2007. *Making a Difference in the Lives of Bilingual/Bicultural Children.* New York: Peter Lang.

Souto-Manning, Mariana. 2007. "Immigrant Families and Children (Re)Develop Identities in a New Context." *Early Childhood Education Journal* 34(6): 399–405.

Souto-Manning, Mariana, and Kevin Swick. 2006. "Teachers' Beliefs About Parent and Family Involvement: Rethinking Our Family Involvement Paradigm." *Early Childhood Education Journal* 34(2): 187–93.

Stipek, Deborah. 2006. "No Child Left Behind Comes to Preschool." *Elementary School Journal* 106(5): 455–66.

Swick, Kevin. 2004. "What Parents Seek in Relations with Early Childhood Family Helpers." *Early Childhood Education Journal* 31(3): 217–20.

Taylor, Benjamin, Sarah Gershon, and Adrian Pantoja. 2012. "Christian America? Understanding the Link Between Church and Attitudes and 'Being American' Among Latino Immigrants." Paper presented at the annual meeting of the American Political Science Association. New Orleans (August 30–September 2).

Tobin, Joseph. 2000. *Good Guys Don't Wear Hats: Children's Talk About the Media.* New York: Teachers College Press.

Tobin, Joseph, Yeh Hsueh, and Mayumi Karasawa. 2009. *Preschool in Three Cultures Revisited: China, Japan, and the United States.* Chicago: University of Chicago Press.

Tobin, Joseph, David Wu, and Dana Davidson. 1989. *Preschool in Three Cultures: Japan, China, and the United States.* New Haven, Conn.: Yale University Press.

Tse, Lucy. 2001. *Why Don't They Learn English? Separating Fact from Fallacy in the U.S. Language Debate.* New York: Teachers College Press.

Valdez, Guadalupe. 1996. *Con Respeto: Bridging the Distances Between Culturally Diverse Families and Schools.* New York: Teachers College Press.

Valenzuela, Angela, and Sanford Dornbusch. 1994. "Familism and Social Capital in the Academic Achievement of Mexican Origin and Anglo Adolescents." *Social Science Quarterly* 75(1): 18–36.

Vandenbroeck, Michel. 2009. "Let Us Disagree." *European Early Childhood Research Journal* 17(2): 165–70.

Vandenbroeck, Michel, Griet Roets, and Aisja Snoeck. 2009. "Immigrant Mothers Crossing Borders: Nomadic Identities and Multiple Belongings in Early Childhood Education." *European Early Childhood Research Journal* 17(2): 203–16.

Vernon-Feagans, Lynne. 1996. *Children's Talk in Communities and Classrooms.* Cambridge, Mass.: Blackwell.

Villenas, Sofia. 2002. "Reinventing Education in New Latino Communities: Pedagogies of Change and Continuity in North Carolina." In *Education in the New Latino Diaspora*, edited by Stanton Wortham, Enrique G. Murillo Jr., and Edmund T. Hamann. Westport, Conn.: Greenwood Publishing.

Waters, Mary. 1999. *Black Identities: West Indian Immigrant Dreams and American Realities.* New York: Russell Sage Foundation.

Whiting, Beatrice, and Carolyn Edwards. 1988. *Children of Different Worlds.* Cambridge, Mass.: Harvard University Press.

Wong, Janelle, Kathy Rim, and Haven Perez. 2008. Protestant Churches and Conservative Politics: Latinos and Asians in the United States." In *Civic Hopes and Political Realities: Immigrants, Community Organizations, and Political Engagement*, edited by S. Karthick Ramakrishnan and Irene Bloemraad. New York: Russell Sage Foundation.

Wright, Wayne. 2005. "The Political Spectacle of Arizona's Proposition 203." *Educational Policy* 19(5): 662–700.

Yafeh, Orit. 2007. "The Time in the Body: Cultural Construction of Femininity in Ultraorthodox Kindergartens for Girls." *Ethos* 35(4): 516–53.

Yaglom, Miriam. 1993. "Role of Psychocultural Factors in the Adjustment of Soviet Jewish Refugees: Applying Kleinian Theory of Mourning." *Journal of Contemporary Psychology* 23(2): 135–45.

Yoshikawa, Hirokazu. 2012. *Immigrants Raising Citizens: Undocumented Parents and Their Young Children.* New York: Russell Sage Foundation.

Yosso, Tara. 2002. "Toward a Critical Race Curriculum." *Equity and Excellence in Education* 35(2): 93–107.

Zigler, Edward, and Karen Anderson. 1979. "An Idea Whose Time had Come: The Intellectual and Political Climate for Head Start." In *Project Head Start: A Legacy of the War on Poverty*, edited by Edward Zigler and Jeanette Valentine. New York: The Free Press.

Index

Boldface numbers refer to figures and tables.

abortion, 10
academic achievement: and bilingual programs, 69; Mexican immigrant children, 23, 109; and preschool attendance, 18
academic curriculum: criticisms of, 42–43; immigrant parents' desire for, 1, 4–5, 12, 40–45
acculturation, 81
Addams, Jane, 3, 6
adult authority, 86–89
African Americans: curriculum preferences, 42, 57; oppositional youth culture, 81; tension with African immigrants, 101–2
African immigrants, 101–2. See also specific groups
Akhtar, Salman, 90–91
Amanti, Cathy, 121
American culture, negative features of, 80–82
Americanization, 3–4
anti-immigrant attitudes, 5, 13. See also prejudice
Anzaldú, Gloria, 97
Arizona: anti-immigration legislation,

32; English-language-only programs, 4; immigrant community, 32; immigrant parents' curriculum views, 35–36, 37, 39–40; language instruction, 60–62; racism, 98–99. See also Phoenix, Ariz.
assimilation, 19, 23, 81

Ballenger, Cynthia, 22
Bank Street College, 34
bathroom use, 83, 123
best practice, 12, 13, 14
bicultural or bilingual teachers and staff members: Head Start programs, 34; immigrant parents' desire for, 72–74; parent-teacher liaisons, 128; role of, 17–18, 111–15
bilingualism and bilingual education: criticisms of, 67–69; decline in, 4; immigrant parents' support for, 59, 64–70; in Iowa, 76–77; research findings, 63, 69; teachers' lack of training, 74–76
Bosnian immigrants, 40, 41

California: English-language-only programs, 4; Head Start enrollment, 20

Caribbean immigrants, 81, 87, 102
Catholic preschools, 42
Chavez, Cesar, 97
Chicago, Ill., early childhood education assumptions, 3
Chicano identity, 96–97
Chicanos Por La Causa, 34
child care, 18–19, 20
child development, 14, 114–15
Children Crossing Borders research project: focus of, 2; limitations of, 28–30; methodology, 2–3, 22–30. *See also specific site locations*
citizenship, 19
class, 9–10, 56–57
coding, 30
communication, 14–16, 119–20, 126–28
community context, 8–9, 21–23, 30–34
comparative approaches, 22
conservatism: in Europe, 86; of immigrant parents, 9–11, 42–43; multiculturalism critiques, 5
constructivism: class-based differences, 42–43; criticisms of, 42; cultural differences, 42–43; developmentally appropriate practice, 44; NAEYC standards, 56; teachers' commitment to, 12, 54–55; Upper West Side Head Start program, 34
contact zones: identity in, 89, 94–95; prejudice and discrimination experiences, 103, 116
content analysis, 30
conversion narratives, 43–44, 54
core knowledge, 42
Crosnoe, Robert, 23
cultural negotiation, 119–20
cultural sensitivity and responsiveness: vs. curriculum best practice, 12, 53; Head Start standards, 16; NAEYC standards, 16; research findings, 115

cultural traditions, 89–90, 94
cultural values: accommodations for, 12; communal or family-oriented perspective, 110; and early childhood education perspectives, 9–10; gender distinctions, 82–84; home culture preservation, 5, 80–82, 88–89; idealization of home culture, 89–92
culture war, 42
curriculum, 35–58; as battleground issue, 4–5; beliefs based on social class, 56–57; cultural sensitivity and responsiveness, 12, 16, 53, 115; immigrant parents' views, 1–2, 35–40; "middle path" approaches, 56; teachers' feelings of threats to professionalism, 53–55; teachers' views, 2, 5, 44–53, 57–58. *See also* academic curriculum; play-based curriculum

DAP (developmentally appropriate practices), 44–45
data analysis, 30
Davidson, Dana, 23
deference, 110–11, 126
deficit perspective: Head Start curriculum, 119; immigrant parents viewed through, 3, 55, 58; Mexican immigrant children viewed through, 109
Delgado-Gaitan, Concha, 22
Delpit, Lisa, 42
democracy, 121
developmentally appropriate practices (DAP), 44–45
dialogue, teacher-parent, 14–16, 126–28
didactic instruction, 42–43, 51
direct instruction: class-based differences in preference for, 57; criticisms of, 42; cultural differences in preference for, 42–43; immigrant parents' desire for, 1; Islamic tradition, 50
discipline, 86–89

discrimination: in Arizona, 98–99; coping mechanisms, 89; in Iowa, 89, 105, 117. *See also* prejudice
diversity, 4
Dominican immigrants, 65, 67
Dornbusch, Sanford, 22
Doucet, Fabienne, 15, 120
Duron, Carmen, 121–22

Early, Diane, 34
early childhood education: history of, 3; immigrant incorporation role, 3–4; literature review, 21–23. *See also specific index headings*
ecological decisionmaking, 8–9, 40–41
ecological framework, 22
economic outcomes, 18
educators. *See* teachers
Egyptian immigrants, 79–80, 82, 102
English-language learners (ELLs), 13, 18
English-language-only programs: in Arizona, 60–61; immigrant parents' support for, 7, 67–70; shift from bilingual programs to, 4, 60–61
English-language proficiency, 92–93
enrollment trends, 2, 21
ethnic enclaves, 92–96, 103
ethnic identity. *See* identity
ethnography, multi-sited, 2, 22–23
evangelical Christians, 10

family-oriented culture, 110
family support workers, 113, 128
fatalism, 126
fear, 126
Filipino immigrants, 40
first-language retention, 64–67, 69, 71–72
Florida, universal preschool in, 10
focus group interviews, 2, 26–30, **31**
Foner, Nancy, 22, 101–2

food, 90–91, 123–24
French preschools, 28, 113–14
Fuller, Bruce, 22–23, 43
funding issues, 18
Funds of Knowledge, 121

Gallimore, Ronald, 22, 74
gay marriage, 10
gender, 82–84, 124
geographical differences, 8–9
Georgia, universal preschool in, 10
Gogolin, Ingrid, 69
Goldenberg, Claude, 22, 74
Gomez, Lolie, 25–26, 63–64, 121–24
González, Norma, 121
Guatemalan immigrants, 43, 123

Haitian immigrants, 22
Harlem Head Start: cultural values, 81; focus group interviews, 26, **29**, 32; home-language retention, 65; parents' curriculum views, 39; prejudice, 100–101, 103; research setting, 2–3; teachers' curriculum views, 46, 49
Harwood, Robin, 88
Head Start: California enrollment trends, 20; comparisons with state programs, 33–34; cultural responsiveness, 16; immigrant enrollment, 21; immigrant teachers, 17, 54; mission of, 11; parental involvement, 118–19; poverty issue, 11–12; prejudice issue, 11–12; program variation, 34. *See also* Harlem Head Start; Queen Creek Head Start program; Upper West Side Head Start
home-language retention, 64–67, 69, 71–72
Honduran immigrants, 87
Hsueh, Yeh, 42
Hull House, 3

identity, 79–116; and adult authority, 86–89; and bicultural staff, 111–15; concerns about, 97–99; in ethnic enclaves, 92–96; gender distinctions, 82–84; idealization of home culture, 89–92; introduction, 79–80; of Mexican immigrants, 96–97; and prejudice, 99–111; religious education, 84–86. *See also* multiculturalism

immigrant children: preschool enrollment, 2; statistics, 2, 20

immigrant parents: communication with teachers, 14–16, 119–20, 126–28; conservatism of, 9–11, 42–43; curriculum views, 1–2, 4–5, 12, 35–45; desire for bicultural or bilingual teachers and staff, 72–74; focus groups, 26–28; involvement in school, 117–28; listening to, 14; parenting style, 86–89; voice of, 14–16

incorporating immigrants into the host society, role of early childhood education, 3–4

information, access to, 9

Iowa: bilingualism battle, 76–77; bilingual staff members, 113; cultural values, 88, 95; demographics, 33; focus group interviews, 27–28, **29, 31,** 33; gender distinctions, 84; home-language retention, 65, 67; identity, 80, 97; immigrant children attending preschools, 20; language instruction, 64, 70, 71; parental involvement, 117–18; parents' curriculum views, 36, 37–38; prejudice, 103, 105–9; racism, 89; research setting, 2; teachers' curriculum views, 45–46, 48–49; teachers' preparation for working with immigrants, 13

Islam, 85–86, 102–3

Islamic preschools, 42

Islamic School (Tempe): cultural values, 82–83; focus group interviews, **29, 31,** 32; parent demographics, 32; parents' curriculum views, 37, 39; prejudice experiences, 11; religious education, 85–86; teachers' curriculum views, 49–51

Italian preschools, 28, 83, 123

Ivorian immigrants, 67, 85

Japanese preschools, 123

Jewish preschools, 42

Karasawa, Mayumi, 23, 42

kindergarten readiness: English proficiency, 4, 60–61, 70; immigrant parents' concerns, 1, 7, 41, 51; teachers' role, 47–48, 49

Kymlicka, Will, 69

La India María, 98

language, 59–78; barriers, 125–26; as battleground issue, 4; home-language retention, 64–67, 69, 71–72; parental pragmatism about, 69–70; responsibility of parents vs. schools, 71–72; stereotypes, 109; teachers' instruction approaches, 60–64. *See also* bilingualism and bilingual education; English-language-only programs

La Raza, 16

Lareau, Annette, 42, 43

Latino immigrant children: population statistics, 20; preschool enrollment, 21

Latinos: academic achievement, 23; early childhood education expectations, 22; gender roles and distinctions, 83–84; parenting style, 88. *See also specific groups*

legal status, 9–10, 21

LeVine, Robert, 89

Lightfoot, Dory, 6, 119

Lissak, Rivka, 3, 6

Los Angeles, Calif., early childhood
    education expectations study, 22
Los Lobos, 97
Louie, Vivian, 43

machismo, 83–84
Mahalingam, Ramaswami, 83
Malian immigrants, 85, 87
Malinche, 91–92
manners, 85–86
Maori, Te Whariki national early child-
    hood education framework, 15–16
melting pot, 79
Mesa, Ariz.: cultural traditions, 95; cur-
    riculum, 35–36; focus group, 32; lan-
    guage, 71–72; nostalgia for home
    country, 91; prejudice, 103–4
methodology, 2–3, 22–30
Mexican Americans, curriculum pref-
    erences, 42
Mexican immigrants: academic
    achievement, 23; adult authority, 86–
    87; bilingual teachers, 72–74; cultural
    traditions, 89–90, 95; curriculum
    views, 1, 35–38, 41, 43–44; early
    childhood education views, 21–22;
    English-language learning, 70; gen-
    der distinctions, 83–84; identity,
    96–97; language instruction, 71;
    nostalgia for home country, 90–92;
    prejudice against, 102, 103–9; Span-
    ish retention, 64–65; values, 88–89
"middle path" curriculum approaches,
    56
Mixtec-speaking immigrants, 33, 66–
    67, 95
modeling, 64
modesty, 82–83, 123
Moll, Luis, 121
monolingual programs, 69–70
Monroe Head Start. See Upper West
    Side Head Start

Moraga, Cherie, 91, 97
moral values: and curriculum views,
    42–43; religious schools, 84–86, 115–
    16; and selective acculturation, 81
Morton, Rebecca, 43
Mouffe, Chantal, 121
mourning, 91
multiculturalism: criticisms of, 5; Head
    Start principles, 16; immigrant par-
    ents' view of, 7; vs. incorporation
    policy, 4. See also identity
multi-sited approach, 2, 22–23
Muscatine, Iowa, 105–6
Muslims, 85–86, 102–3. See also Islamic
    School (Tempe)

NAEYC (National Association for the
    Education of Young Children), 16,
    44, 56
names, 109, 112
naptime, 120
Nashville, Tenn.: demographics, 33; fo-
    cus group interviews, 29, 31, 33;
    identity, 80; language instruction,
    61–63; population distribution by
    race and ethnicity, 33; prejudice, 105;
    research setting, 2; teachers' curricu-
    lum views, 46, 47–48; teachers' prep-
    aration for working with immigrants,
    13
National Association for the Education
    of Young Children (NAEYC), 16, 44,
    56
National Institute of Child Health and
    Human Development (NICHD),
    Study of Early Child Care and Youth
    Development, 23
National Research Council, 119
National Taskforce for the Early Edu-
    cation of Hispanics, 23
New York City: bilingual education,
    68; child rearing strategies study, 22;

New York City (*cont.*)
cultural values, 82; demographics, 32; early childhood education assumptions, 3; focus group interviews, **29, 31,** 32; identity, 80; immigrant parents' curriculum views, 39, 43; research setting, 2–3; teachers' curriculum views, 45, 46–47; teachers' preparation for working with immigrants, 13. *See also* Harlem Head Start; Upper West Side Head Start

New Zealand, Te Whariki national early childhood education framework, 15–16

NICHD (National Institute of Child Health and Human Development), Study of Early Child Care and Youth Development, 23

No Child Left Behind Act (2001), 4, 45, 76–77

nostalgia, 90–91

Oklahoma, universal preschool in, 10

oppositional youth culture, 81

oppression, 55

Pakistani immigrants, 39, 80–81, 102–3

parental involvement, 117–28; barriers to, 14, 125–26; divergent interests of parents and teachers, 120–21; forms of, 118; in Head Start programs, 118–19; implementation challenges, 6; importance of, 5–6; parent-teacher dialogue, 119–20, 126–28; Solano Preschool program, 121–26; suggestions for, 124–25; teacher's defensiveness, 117

parenting style, 86–89

parents, immigrant. *See* immigrant parents

parent-teacher conferences, 74

patriotism, 89–90

Pease-Alvarez, Lucinda, 22, 70

Perez, Haven, 33

personal names, 109, 112

Phoenix, Ariz.: adult authority, 86–87; cultural traditions, 90; demographics, 32; focus group interviews, **29,** 30–32; home-language retention, 66–67; identity, 80, 92–95; language instruction, 71–72, 77; prejudice, 11, 100, 103, 104; research setting, 2; teachers' curriculum views, 45; teachers' preparation for working with immigrants, 13. *See also* Islamic School (Tempe); Queen Creek Head Start program; Solano Preschool

Piaget, Jean, 45

Pianta, Robert, 34

play-based curriculum: conversion narratives, 43–44; criticisms of, 42–43; immigrant parents' views, 1–2, 4–5, 35–40; teachers' support of, 4–5, 12

policy issues, Americanization vs. multiculturalism, 3–4

political beliefs, and early childhood education perspectives, 9–10

population statistics, 2, 20

Portes, Alejandro, 22, 23, 43, 81, 84, 89

poverty, 11–12, 100

pragmatism, 7–8, 40–41, 69–70

Preissing, Christa, 128

prejudice: experiences of, 11–12, 99–109; responses to, 110–11. *See also* discrimination

Preschool in Three Cultures Revisited (Yeh and Karasawa), 23

preschools: and citizenship, 19; enrollment trends, 2, 21; history of, 3; immigrant incorporation role, 3–4; literature review, 21–23; universal programs, 10; value to immigrant

children and families, 18–19. *See also
specific index headings*
*Preschools in Three Cultures: Japan,
China, and the United States* (Tobin,
Wu, and Davidson), 23
privacy, 83, 123
private preschools, 21
professionalism, teachers' feelings of
threats to, 53–55

quality, 34
Queen Creek Head Start program: cultural sensitivity, 95; demographics,
32; home-language retention, 66–67;
identity, 97, 98; program philosophy,
34

Race to the Top Early Learning Challenge Grant, 16
racial identity. *See* identity
racism, 89, 98–99
Reese, Leslie, 22
religious schools, 42, 84–86
religious values: accommodations for,
12; and early childhood education
perspectives, 9–10; education in, 84–
86
Rim, Kathy, 33

Santa Ana, Otto, 104
Saudi immigrants, 39
scaffolding, 56
segmented assimilation, 23, 81
selective acculturation, 81
self-fulfilling prophecies, 109
Senegalese immigrants, 85, 87
Small, Mario, 127
social class, 9–10, 56–57
social isolation, 126
Solano Preschool: bilingual staff members, 72; curriculum, 25–26; focus
group interviews, **29, 31**; funding,

25; parental involvement program,
121–26; parents' curriculum views,
35–36, 43–44; student demographics,
25, 32; video, 25–26
Somali immigrants, 89, 103
Souto-Manning, Mariana, 109
Spanish language: instruction in, 25–
26, 60–64; interviews conducted in,
27; retention of, 64–67, 71–72; stereotypes, 109
Spanish-speaking immigrants. *See specific groups*
Standardized Childhoods (Fuller), 22–23
standards, 16
stigmatization, 11, 103
stress, 126
Sudanese immigrants, 36, 84, 88, 95–96
superiority, 89

teacher-parent dialogue, 14–16, 126–28
teachers: communication with parents,
14–16, 119–20, 126–28; cultural sensitivity, 12; curriculum views, 1–2, 5,
44–53, 57–58; feelings of threats to
professionalism, 53–55; focus
groups, 28; lack of preparation for
working with immigrants, 12–13;
language instruction, 60–64; prejudice and stereotyping, 105, 108–9;
training, 12–13. *See also* bicultural
or bilingual teachers and staff members
teacher's aides, 106–7
teaching methods, 42–43. *See also* constructivism; direct instruction
Tempe Islamic School. *See* Islamic
School (Tempe)
Te Whariki national early childhood
education framework, 15–16
Tobin, Joseph, 23, 42, 123
training, 12–13
translators, 74, 113

Trueba, Henry, 22
Turkish immigrants, 39, 68–69

undocumented immigrants, 9–10
universal preschool, 10, 18, 22–23
Upper West Side Head Start: bicultural staff, 111–12; focus group interviews, **29**, 32; parents' curriculum views, 1, 51; program philosophy, 34; research setting, 2; teachers' curriculum views, 45, 51–52

Valdez, Guadalupe, 21–22, 42, 89
Valens, Richie, 97
Valenzuela, Angela, 22
values. *See* cultural values; moral values
Vandenbroeck, Michel, 15, 55, 120, 128
video-cued multivocal ethnography, 2, 23–26
Villenas, Sofia, 111
voice of immigrant parents, 14–16
voting, 10–11
Vygotsky, Lev, 45

Waters, Mary, 81, 87
West African immigrants: and African Americans, 81; curriculum views, 39, 41; discipline, 87; prejudice against, 103
West Indian immigrants, 81, 87, 102
West Virginia, universal preschool in, 10
White, Merry, 89
Wong, Janelle, 33
Woods, Robert A., 3
working class, curriculum preferences, 57
Wu, David, 23

Yeh, Hsueh, 23
Yemeni immigrants, 85
Yoshikawa, Hirokazu, 9–10, 22
Yuma, Ariz., 92–93

Zhou, Min, 22, 23, 43, 84, 89